S0-AQE-396

MONARCH
PRESS

Selling Your Home $weet Home

Sloan Bashinsky

MONARCH PRESS | *New York*

Published by Monarch Press
A Division of Simon & Schuster, Inc.
Simon & Schuster Building
Rockefeller Center
1230 Avenue of the Americas
New York, New York 10020

Published by arrangement with Menasha Ridge Press

Manufactured in the United States of America

10 9 8 7 6 5 4 3 2 1

Library of Congress No. 85-50558

ISBN: 0-671-60213-6

To the real estate industry
and its members
for continuing to inspire me to write,
and to my few remaining
real estate and lawyer friends
for their critiques and
for having stood by me.

Contents

Acknowledgements ix
Preface xiii
Introduction: Six Tales of Woe 3

Part 1—The Game: A Seller's Point of View

1 The Buyer 11
2 The Real Estate Agent 15
3 The Lender 23
4 The Closing Agent 35
5 Your Own Representative 37

Part 2—Controlling the Game

6 Pregame Strategy 43
7 Preparing the Product 51
8 Asking and Taking Prices 55
9 For Sale by Owner? 59
10 Working with an Agent 63
11 The Contract Negotiations 73
12 Should You Hold Paper? 79
13 Contingency Offers 89
14 Earnest Money and Buyers with Cold Feet 93

15 Little Things Can Hurt 97
16 After Making the Deal 105

Conclusion 109
Appendixes
A. State Regulatory Agencies 111
B. MLS Rules and Regulations 117
C. Code of Ethics 125
D. Estimated Seller's Net 134
E. Sample Grievance Complaint 137
Index 141

Acknowledgments

Once again, I sincerely thank Fred Bonnie, who challenged me to write, Dede Self for typing the manuscript (about a dozen times), and Jane, my wife, who made it all possible.

Disclaimer

My publisher keeps insisting that I qualify the advice I give in my books. So here's another, but fortunately brief, disclaimer.

I have attempted to write this book for national use by people selling their homes. However, there are certain to be local differences in real estate laws, customs and practices that may alter the advice I have given. Furthermore, the federal tax laws have an annoying habit of changing, rendering perfectly good tax advice extinct.

The general principles I have given you are sound, but you had better check with a good real estate lawyer, broker or agent in your area about local variations and current tax laws.

Preface

I am basically a home buyer's representative, because few lawyers or real estate agents where I live care to represent home buyers. But I do represent sellers from time to time, and I have been involved in hundreds of sales of traditional and condominium homes as the closing agent or the representative of either the buyer or the seller. As you can imagine, I have seen many unfortunate things happen to both buyers and sellers.

My critical view of the home buying process is expressed in my first book, *HOME BUYERS: Lambs to the Slaughter?* If you will be buying another home after selling your present one, then you might want to read *Lambs to the Slaughter?* Even if you will not be buying another home you might want to read it, because it will give you a clear view of what an aggressive buyer might do to you.

As to selling a home, it has been my experience that sellers often come up short due to their lack of understanding of the home buying/selling process, lack of assertiveness (wanting to be nice) and/or having placed too much trust in a real estate agent. Much has been written about selling a home, but not about how to do it without being taken advantage of. With that in mind, I will now lead you through the business of selling a home in a way never before presented.

Selling Your Home
$weet Home

Introduction: Six Tales of Woe

I can think of no better way to explain what can happen to you selling a home than to begin with a few real-life adventures. Throughout this book, I will refer back to these tales by the seller's name, i.e., "The Accountant's Father," to make a point. Therefore, it probably will be helpful for you to thoroughly familiarize yourself with these sad-but-true stories before reading further.

The Accountant's Father

I once gave a talk to a group of women certified public accountants. The young woman who was to introduce me told me beforehand about the time that her father sold his home. The story went like this:

Her father listed his home for sale with a woman real estate agent who was a friend of the family. She asked him what was the lowest amount he would take for his home, and he suggested a figure several thousand dollars below the list (asking) price. The first offer he got was for precisely what he had said he would take. His agent friend told him that the buyer was also interested in another home and that he should accept the initial offer or risk losing the buyer. She also reminded him that the offer was one he had indicated a willingness to accept. So my friend's father accepted the offer, and his agent received a full 6 percent commission at the closing for "negotiating" the sale.

Jan

In another case, a young divorcee, Jan, was forced by financial problems to sell her home. Two days before the closing, she learned that she was going to be charged an unexpected $1,800 for paying off her home loan early. She came to me to see if I could do something about it.

Her loan documents clearly provided for a prepayment penalty. So I called her agent. "Who would have ever thought there would be a prepayment penalty" the agent exclaimed. Since the agent had not checked the loan documents before putting the home on the market, I advised Jan to reduce the real estate commission by the amount of the prepayment penalty, which the lending company was clearly due. She said she couldn't do that because the agent was a friend.

The Elderly Couple

In this case, an elderly couple came to me after agreeing to sell their home of over thirty years. The contract drawn by their agent was contingent on the buyer obtaining "necessary financing" (whatever that meant), and the closing was to be some four months later, *if* the buyer got his financing. Furthermore, the couple had also agreed to deliver possession on the date of closing, meaning they were to have packed, sold or otherwise removed belongings accumulated over thirty years or longer without being sure that they had their home sold. Finally, if the buyer could not secure his financing, they would have lost four of the best selling months.

I luckily got this one worked out by getting the buyer to agree to define his financing and to a shorter time within which he was to get it. He also agreed to allow my clients to pay rent and stay in their home an extra thirty days after the closing, so they could wait to pack up until they were sure their home was sold.

The agent had clearly drafted a sloppy contract, which caused the couple a lot of anxiety and led them to hire a lawyer. I suggested to them that they reduce the commission enough to cover my fee and the rent they would pay. They thought it a grand idea and did it. The look on the agent's face was memorable.

The Brights

In this case, a young couple, the Brights, sold their home. The contract of sale drawn up by the buyer's agent stated that the property was not located in a floodplain. Two years earlier, unknown to the Brights, the home had been designated as being in a floodplain. The agent with the listing on the Bright's home was not aware of the floodplain designation and allowed them to accept the buyer's offer as written.

About a year after the closing, the sheriff delivered suit papers accusing them of misrepresentations and claiming $50,000 in damages. That was when the Brights first learned of the new floodplain designation.

The agents had failed to check the city records about the floodplain. A simple phone call would have gotten the information. So, I asked the agents and their firms to defend and hold the Brights harmless in the suit, reasoning that the agents' negligence had caused the whole thing. This request was denied, and now the Brights are faced with spending several thousand dollars defending the suit, in which they also will sue the agents and their firms.

The Poors

The next case is about a couple named Poor who had sold a home to a couple named Wilt, taking back a large twenty-year second mortgage with a balloon provision in it saying that the entire amount would be due and payable in three years. The Poors' agent had assured them that the Wilts would be able to refinance within three years and pay off the mortgage. Of course, the agent got cash, not a mortgage, for the commission at the closing.

The Poors then bought another home using the same method of financing, thinking that when the Wilts paid them, they would pay their sellers. Three years passed, and the Wilts were not able to refinance, and still haven't been able to do it. I was able to buy a two-year extension by getting the Poors' seller to accept $2,000 from the Wilts, but the time bomb is still ticking.

The Nathans

How about one more? A young couple, the Nathans, were moving out of town. They listed their home for sale through an agent of a local real estate firm. This agent I will call the listing agent.

Several months passed and nothing happened. Then, about six weeks before they were to move, the Nathans received and accepted an offer presented by an agent of another real estate firm. I will call this agent the buyer's agent. However, both agents were legally the Nathans' agents, because the Nathans were paying the sales commission.

About two weeks before the deal was to close, the buyer changed his mind and asked his agent if he could back out of the deal. Without consulting with the listing agent or the Nathans, the buyer's agent told him he could get out of the deal by forfeiting his earnest money deposit of $1,000. This was acceptable to the buyer, and his agent then notified the listing agent that the deal was off.

The terms of the sales contract and state law, however, gave the Nathans the option of bringing a lawsuit to force the buyer to close. In other words, the Nathans did not have to agree to the forfeiture of the earnest money deposit. The buyer's agent knew this but did not like doing things that way. Furthermore, she and the buyer were old friends. The listing agent's broker knew of this option, though, and referred the Nathans to me. I explained their legal rights to them. They felt that they had no alternative under the circumstances and instructed me to force the buyer to close.

Unfortunately, the buyer, thinking he could get out of the Nathans' contract, had agreed to buy a condominium. Having changed his position on advice of one of the seller's agents, he had a legal defense to the lawsuit. I felt that he did not know this, though, and threatened to file suit immediately. I also told the brokers of each real estate firm that, if the deal didn't close, the Nathans would hold the buyer's agent and her firm responsible.

About this time, the listing agent became very upset—she didn't like the lawsuit idea either—and repeatedly tried to get the Nathans to fire me and put their home back on the market. I advised the listing agent's broker what his agent was doing and asked him to stop it. He said that he would not unless the Nathans personally requested him to do so. So, I had the Nathans call him, and he told his agent to back off.

Finally, the buyer, I think out of sympathy for "his" agent, agreed to close on the Nathans' home. At my suggestion, the Nathans decided to reduce the real estate commission by the amount of my fee because of the trouble and expense the agents had caused. Furthermore I, not the agents, had brought the buyer to the closing table. The agents and their brokers, with hands out after trying to kill the deal, went berserk, insisting on the *full* commission.

I asked the closing lawyer if he would close and hold back the real estate commission pending a resolution of that issue. The lawyer refused to do this, because both agents sent him a lot of closings and he was afraid of losing their business. So, I made arrangements for another, less sensitive lawyer to close the deal. Then, I informed the agents and their brokers that my clients were going to file a grievance against them with the Real Estate Commission if they caused any more trouble. This got their attention, and they agreed to reduce the commission as requested.

* * * * *

These types of problems come up entirely too often, but, as in the first two tales, most sellers choose not to do anything about them. Remember this fact and these horror stories as we get better acquainted with the characters and learn how to deal with them.

Part 1

The Game: A Seller's Point of View

The principal players in the game of selling your home will be you, who have the product, and your buyer, who has the money to buy it. Three other players you may encounter along the way might be a real estate agent, who finds your buyer for you, a commercial lender, who lends your buyer the money to buy your home, and the closing agent, who closes the deal and pays you the buyer's money.

It would appear on the surface that you, the real estate agent, lender and closing agent, having the buyer's money as a common goal, will be playing on the same team. This, as demonstrated in the Introduction and following chapters, could be a costly assumption for you to make.

In another vein, your lovely home in all probability will not be as enamoring to your buyer as it is to you. Furthermore, you cannot pick it up and carry it off if you get tired of the game. Your buyer's money, on the other hand, is readily spendable, thus portable. Unlike you, your buyer can get mad, take the ball, go home and end the game.

These will be important facts to remember as we meet and learn how to deal with the characters in the following chapters.

1 *The Buyer*

The buyer is obviously the most important person to you. Without a buyer, there's no sale. So what about this buyer?

Buyer wariness. Buyers will be more at the mercy of the system than you. Although not fully aware of their predicament, most buyers know that they are at a disadvantage and tend to be wary. For that reason, you will not want to do anything that might spook a buyer, such as putting your home on the market without giving a believable reason for doing so—you plan to build another home, move to the country, or something else believable. Otherwise, the buyer might think that you are selling because there is something wrong with your home, neighborhood or school system.

Disclosure requirements. Under the rule of "caveat emptor" (let the buyer beware), you are not required to volunteer anything about your home, neighborhood or whatever to a buyer except serious defects or health hazards that (1) you know exist and (2) are not obvious at the time. A couple of examples of things you must disclose are a septic system that backs up or a basement that floods only during the rainy season. However, if a buyer asks you questions, any answers you give must be (1) the truth and (2) the whole truth. So, if a buyer asks you if your well water is potable and in late summer it isn't, or what school district you are in and you know that it will be different the next fall, then your answer will have to state this fact. If there are things such as this that you do not want a buyer to ask you, try to be absent when the buyer comes around. Don't lie, though, or try to cover up defects, for instance, by painting over a water-damaged wall. If you do, you may well find yourself on the short end of a fraud lawsuit, and juries hate frauds and cheats.

If you are working with a real estate agent, understand that your agent is required by your state's real estate laws to advise a potential buyer of any known serious defects in your home. Agents don't like being sued either, so you can expect your agent to ask you what, if anything, is wrong with your home. This information, as I said, must be passed on to the buyer. If you withhold something about the home from the agent, such as the basement leaks, or, if you don't tell the agent that the school district is being changed, the courts will probably treat this the same as if you held those facts back from the buyer. Then, if the buyer sues, your agent will probably be sued, too, and you can bet your last dollar that your agent will testify against you at the trial to avoid liability.

Buyer games. Buyers will play games with you, such as: not wanting to pay what you think your home is worth; asking you to finance part of the purchase price; wanting you to sell them your home subject to them selling their own, which takes your home off the market without any real assurance that the buyers will close; not telling you that they have a home to sell, while making an offer contingent on their getting financing which they know that they cannot get until they sell their home; changing their minds about wanting your home two months after signing a contract to buy it or getting you to agree to finance part of the purchase price and then not paying you.

Buyers are also real good at getting valuable information about you from your real estate agent. For example, you have already signed a contract to buy another home contingent on your selling the one you now own, and you really want that other home and will do anything to sell the one you now own. You will never know what your agent has told a buyer (remember what happened to The Accountant's Father and the Nathans), and, to me, this is the most maddening thing of all.

I will tell you more about buyers as we work along, but let's turn now to the Real Estate Agent.

2 *The Real Estate Agent*

Most homes are sold using the services of a real estate agent. By law, all real estate agents must work for a licensed real estate firm, and the real estate firm must have a licensed real estate broker who supervises the activities of the firm's agents. When a commission is earned, the agent making the sale gets part of it, say, 60 percent, and the broker's firm gets the rest. All real estate agents and brokers are licensed under and required to obey their state's real estate licensing laws, which are supposed to be enforced by a state real estate regulatory agency.[1]

Realtors® and the Multiple Listing Service. Often the term "Realtor®" is used to describe *any* real estate agent. However, Realtors® are only those real estate agents or brokers who are members of a very large and influential real estate organization (over 600,000 members in 1984) known as the National Association of Realtors® (NAR). So not all real estate agents or brokers are Realtors®, but all Realtors® are real estate agents or brokers.

1. A listing of the state real estate regulatory agencies is furnished in Appendix A.

NAR controls what is called the "Multiple Listing Service" or "MLS."[2] This is a system of information available to participating MLS members, who must be Realtors® in most areas (California is one of the more notable exceptions). The information consists of what homes are listed for sale by MLS subscribers in your community and a description of each home and other data, such as the financing on the home, the school district and so forth. All of this information is used by MLS subscribers to match buyers and sellers of homes, and it is generally thought that MLS is very helpful in doing this.[3]

In addition to offering the Multiple Listing Service, NAR also claims that its members are better trained and more ethical than agents who are not NAR members. In my experience, this is generally true, although it happened that the agents described in the Introduction were Realtors®. More important to you, though, is the fact that NAR usually controls the residential real estate market and the rules of the game, often to your disadvantage. Before explaining what I mean by this, I will first explain the *legal* obligations of an agent.

Fiduciary duty. Under the law, a real estate agent owes what is called a "fiduciary duty" to the person who pays the agent's commission. This is the highest duty of protection imposed by the law and is similar to the duty of protection that a lawyer owes a client. In plain English, if you are paying an agent's commission, then that agent is legally required to try to get you the best possible deal. Note that I said "legally required," for, in practice, this usually does not occur, as demonstrated by what happened to the sellers in the Introduction.

2. For illustration purposes, typical Multiple Listing Service Rules and Regulations are reproduced in Appendix B. The MLS rules for your area can be obtained from your local Board of Realtors® or MLS.

3. However, of the homes listed in MLS in Birmingham, Alabama, for example, in 1983, about 32 percent actually sold that year.

Double agents. Now, back to the point I was making. Agents tend to act as double agents, playing seller and buyer against each other to the agent's advantage. This behavior is, I think, encouraged by NAR's Code of Ethics[4], which sets the standards of the real estate industry. Specifically, Article 7, National Association of Realtors® Code of Ethics states:

> In accepting employment as an agent, the Realtor® pledges himself to protect and promote the interests of the client. This obligation of *absolute fidelity* to the client's interest is *primary*, but it does not relieve the Realtor® of the obligation to *treat fairly* all parties to the transaction. (Emphasis added)

Note that the first sentence of Article 7 states the agent's fiduciary duty. The second sentence follows by describing it as one of absolute fidelity (faithfulness), which it is. Then the second sentence begins to artfully equivocate, relegating the agent's duty to being only primary (therefore, not absolute), then to having to treat all parties fairly. Seems pretty confusing, doesn't it? In fact, you are probably wondering how in the world your agent can try to get you the best possible deal while being fair to the buyer?

To me, the answer is obvious. It cannot be done. But most agents will say that they can do it. In fact, I remember one agent arguing violently with me when I was a guest on a radio call-in program that she, in fact, had a fiduciary duty to both the buyer and the seller in each transaction. Stunned, I asked her how she had arrived at this, and she said that was what she had been taught in her real estate licensing school.

4. The Code of Ethics of the National Association of Realtors® and the Standards of Practice relating thereto are reproduced in Appendix C. These govern the actions of all Realtors®. However, these rules do not override state laws regulating real estate brokers and agents and which apply to all brokers and agents.

On another occasion, an agent friend explained it this way. He said he had a fiduciary duty to the buyer when he was working with a buyer until the buyer made an offer, then he became the agent of the seller and thereafter had a fiduciary duty to the seller. I wondered if he ever explained this to either the seller or buyer. A broker friend explained it yet another way, saying that agents don't know whom they represent, and I suspect that this is often true. But the most telling explanation came from an accountant, who said that agents represent themselves first, last and foremost.

By straddling the fence, working you and the buyer against each other, agents are better able to control the deal and get it closed and themselves paid. And that's all there is to it. Article 7 seems to legitimate this behavior.

Co-oping. The double agent problem is further aggravated by what agents call "co-oping." This occurs when an agent has a home listed for sale and another agent (who can work for the same or another real estate firm) produces a buyer. All agents have an understanding among themselves, required by MLS in most areas, that the listing agent and firm will co-op the sale and split the real estate commission with the other agent and firm. Real estate agents call the second agent either the "co-op" or the "selling" agent. The terms are interchangeable.

A Federal Trade Commission (FTC) study of the real estate industry completed in 1981, but not released until May 1984, found that 74 percent of home sellers and 71 percent of home buyers interviewed thought that the co-op agent was working for the buyer even though they knew that the seller was paying the co-op agent's commission.

However, under MLS rules and listing agreements, the co-op agent is considered to be the subagent of the listing agent's firm and, therefore, the agent of the *seller*. This means that the co-op agent has a fiduciary duty to the seller, not the buyer. If you call your local Board of Realtors®, you will get the same answer: The seller has two agents and the buyer has no agent in a co-op situation. You will probably get some double-talk, too, to the effect that agents have to be "fair" to all parties concerned—a reference, of course, to Article 7. The impossibility of this task is exemplified by what happened to the Nathans, where the co-op agent, in an effort to be fair to the buyer, sold them down the river.

The co-op agent usually acts like the buyer's agent so that the buyer will trust the agent to get the buyer a good deal. One way of establishing this trust is for the co-op agent to pass information about you on to the buyer ("I shouldn't say this, but. . . .") which is illegal, certainly not "fair" to you and can do you a great deal of harm. The co-op agent gets this information from the listing agent, who wants the deal to close just as badly as the co-op agent.

Dealing with the double agent problem. You might be wondering how such behavior is allowed to continue. Well, it's an old system, and change comes very slowly. In fact, I have copies of letters from the head lawyer of the National Association of Realtors® belittling certain NAR members for suggesting that NAR do something to rectify the problem of its members trying to serve two masters. Specifically, it was suggested that an agent not act on a buyer's behalf against a seller unless the buyer is paying the agent separately. In fact, there is a type of agent who will not work with a buyer unless the buyer is paying the agent a commission. This type of agent is discussed at the end of Chapter 10. If, as a seller, you encounter one of these agents, look out. That agent is the buyer's agent, not a co-op agent, and has a fiduciary duty to the buyer. In other words, that agent is trying to get the buyer, not you, the best possible deal, and knows how to do it, too.

In addition, state real estate laws clearly prohibit such

double-dealing, some of the penalties for it being: loss of claim to a commission from the seller, suspension or revocation of the agent's real estate license and fine and/or imprisonment. (I invoked these rules for The Elderly Couple, the Nathans and the Brights.) But the enforcement of these laws is generally left to state regulatory agencies which consist of —you guessed it—real estate brokers who are often members of NAR.

Sometimes, the double agent issue is presented by an irate seller to the courts for resolution. However, the chief beneficiaries of a lawsuit are lawyers. Furthermore, the mental anguish and expense of a seemingly never ending lawsuit leave this course of action to the stout-of-heart and well-heeled.

The only way an agent you are paying can treat all parties fairly, is to try to get you the best possible deal and to tell the buyer that this is what an agent is legally required to do. This disclosure will remove all unfairness from the transaction, but it seldom is made because most agents, as pointed out, want buyers to think they are being protected.

You are responsible for what your agent says and does. Another serious problem that your agent probably will not disclose to you is that, under the law, you are responsible for anything an agent you are paying (the listing or the co-op agent) tells a buyer or fails to tell a buyer if disclosure is legally required. This is so even if you did not authorize it to be said, know it was said or know if it was the truth. This rule nearly let the Nathans' buyer get away and is what got the Brights into trouble over the floodplain designation. They relied on the co-op agent, who drafted the buyer's offer saying that the home was not in a designated flood area. The Brights have no defense to the buyer's lawsuit, which is why they will sue the co-op agent and her firm as well as the listing agent and her firm. Although it did not happen in the Bright's case, their buyer could have chosen to ask the court to rescind the sale (put the parties back into their original positions) rather than asking for damages.

The only way I know to protect yourself in this area is to write something like the following into the sales contract:

> Even though Seller is paying the commission, Buyer understands and agrees that the co-op agent (with whom Buyer has been working) is the agent of Buyer, not Seller, and, further, that Seller is not liable to Buyer for anything the co-op agent says or does.

This only protects you from the co-op agent, but that's the person most likely to cause you problems. You can expect to get a lot of resistance to putting something like this into your contract. One way to minimize the resistance is to add that the co-op agent is not the agent of the listing agent either, which will also protect the listing agent. This is one provision I would absolutely require whenever there is a co-op agent involved.

* * * * *

There are, however, ways to use a real estate agent to your advantage. I will tell you about them and a lot of other things that you will never hear from a typical agent, but next, let's meet the Lender.

3 *The Lender*

Home loans come in two forms, mortgages and deeds of trust, depending on where you live. Although there are legal differences between the two, in practical terms each is a pledge of your home to secure repayment of the money you have borrowed to buy it. To simplify matters, I will refer to home loans as mortgages.

If there is a mortgage against your home, then the owner of the mortgage is the first lender that will concern you. So, get out your loan documents and let's look at them.

Prepayment penalties. Do the loan documents allow your lender to charge you a penalty for paying off the loan early? Your loan will be paid off early if your buyer obtains a new first mortgage or pays you cash for your home. There will probably be an "implied" prepayment penalty, unless your loan documents state that you can pay off the loan early without penalty. The reason for this is that the lender normally can refuse early payment, unless the payment includes all of the interest that the lender would have earned over the life of the loan. Fortunately, there are loans which do not have prepayment penalties.

For instance, there is no prepayment penalty for Veteran's Administration (VA) loans. There is a penalty of thirty-days interest on Federal Housing Administration (FHA) loans, if you do not give one month's advance written notice of your intent to prepay. And you will be charged a full month's interest on any FHA loan closed on or after the first of the month, so plan to close and pay off the FHA loan by the end of the month. If you are careful, you can avoid the FHA prepayment penalty.

Many conventional loans provide that the penalty only applies if you pay off the loan with funds you have borrowed from another source and not if you pay it off with funds you have received from having sold your home. To be sure, though, request a written statement from your lender now. For, if there is a prepayment penalty, you will want to know how much it is before you decide what to ask for or how to sell you home. Otherwise, you may end up like Jan.

If market interest rates are above the rate that you are paying your lender, then you may be able to get a prepayment penalty waived or reduced, because the lender will be able to turn around and loan the money out at a higher rate of interest. If market rates are substantially higher than the rate you are paying, you may be able to get your lender to discount the loan (accept less than what is owed as payment in full). However, the amount of any such discount will be taxable to you as ordinary income, which reduces its value.

To get a prepayment penalty waived or reduced or a loan discounted, approach your lender now. State that you are in a position to pay off the loan early and, since market rates are higher than you are paying, it will be to your lender's advantage to work a deal with you. Try to avoid disclosing that you are putting your home on the market. If you are using an agent, tell the agent what you are trying to do and to not contact your lender until you give the green light to do so. Otherwise, your agent will let your lender know that you are selling before you are ready. And by all means, do not wait until after the lender knows that you already have an agreement to sell your home. At that point in time you will have no bargaining power, for your lender will know that full payment plus any applicable prepayment penalty will be forthcoming soon enough.

One last point is that you should get any such agreement in writing. Otherwise, you risk the lender having a change of heart after you find your buyer and have lost your bargaining power. Verbal agreements of this nature, though legal in most states, are very hard to prove.

Alienation clauses. You will also want to know if your loan documents contain something called an "alienation" clause. These clauses are inserted into loan documents to prevent you from passing on a low interest, fixed rate loan to someone else (called an "equity sale") during periods of higher interest rates. FHA and VA loans, fortunately, do not contain these clauses.

Alienation clauses come in two basic forms: first, those that give your lender the right to raise the interest rate, charge a large transfer fee and approve your buyer's credit and, second, those that require full payment of the loan if you sell your home (called "due-on-sale" clauses). Alienation clauses can kill an equity sale.

The first type of alienation clause was made popular under the name "Paragraph 17," that being the paragraph number of the form mortgage in which it first appeared. Paragraph 17 revolutionized the lending business and its wording is found in almost all conventional mortgages.

The Federal National Mortgage Association, commonly known as Fannie Mae, is the largest single "investor" in Paragraph 17 type mortgages. It and other investors purchase these mortgages from commercial lenders, which then collect the monthly payments for the investors.

In 1983, Fannie Mae and many other investors adopted a

policy of treating all Paragraph 17 mortgages as being *due-on-sale*, which came as news to every real estate lawyer, real estate agent and mortgage lender in the country. It also came as a rude shock to people who owned a home with a Paragraph 17 mortgage, because they had been told when they bought that they had a renegotiable mortgage—one where the interest rate would be renegotiated on an equity sale to a credit-worthy buyer.

I and most real estate lawyers with whom I have discussed this due-on-sale policy feel that it is illegal and a mere bluff. In other words, it is just an attempt to gouge the unknowledgeable seller (and buyer) that will not be carried through if you hold your ground. Although it is only a hunch, I think what was behind this policy change was the thought of being able to get the seller to pay a prepayment penalty and the buyer to refinance and pay several points, rather than the paltry one point that most commercial lenders were getting on equity sales. (Points are explained later in this chapter.)

If your loan documents contain an alienation clause, get a letter now from your lender stating its requirements on an equity sale. If you are faced with a straight due-on-sale clause, the lender may still allow the sale if you agree to an increase in the interest rate, a transfer fee and a credit check on your buyer. Regardless, you will need this information to decide the price and best way to market your home, and any prospective equity buyer will want to know what the new interest rate, mortgage payment and transfer fee will be on an equity sale.

I have known of many instances where there was an alienation clause and the seller and buyer tried to disguise or pull off an equity sale without notifying the lender. If you do this and the lender later finds out what has happened, you and the buyer will have a big problem. The lender can choose to (1) foreclose, (2) extract a large price from the buyer in the form of an interest rate increase and transfer fee or (3) sue you for the total amount due. If you are holding paper and the lender chooses to foreclose, you will be cut off. If you think that you might want to try it anyway, get a good real estate lawyer, who may be able to give you some tips on how to best protect yourself and not get caught with your hands in the cookie jar.

If your loan does not contain an alienation clause, then you will be able to arrange an equity sale with no interference from your lender. You may also want to use this fact to get your lender to discount your mortgage, if you pay it off instead of selling your equity. Many lenders would prefer to take less than what is owed now, rather than collect it later at a below market rate of interest.

One final thing about alienation clauses. I have known of many cases where one did not exist but the lender tried to create one out of thin air. Any lender that tries this is only bluffing. There is no telling how many unsuspecting sellers have fallen for this, though.

The buyer's financing. The second lender you should know about is the one who loans your buyer new money to buy your home. This lender might be you, or it might be a commercial source of money such as a bank, a savings and loan association or a commercial lending company.

Holding paper. When you let the buyer pay what is due you over a period of time, i.e., you loan the buyer money, it is called "holding paper." There are several ways you could hold paper, each depending on certain facts. Three of the more common situations are given below. Assume in each case a $70,000 sales price and a $10,000 cash down payment.

1. If you own your home free and clear of any mortgages,

you can take $10,000 down and a $60,000 mortgage from the buyer.

2. Your buyer can get a $50,000 new mortgage from a commercial lender such as a bank and give you a $10,000 second mortgage and $10,000 in cash.
3. If you have, say, a $50,000 mortgage, your buyer can take it over (an equity sale) and give you a $10,000 second mortgage and $10,000 in cash.

Holding paper has pluses and minuses. Some of the more obvious minuses are: not getting paid (like the Poors); not getting enough cash to buy your next home or having your money tied up for a long time, usually at a below market rate of interest, which has the effect of reducing what you really get paid. But holding paper can help you sell your home, especially in a slow real estate market. Not only can you give the buyer a lower interest rate and make it easier for the buyer to afford the home, the large costs of getting a loan through commercial channels can be avoided, resulting in part or all of the savings ending up in your pocket instead.

Furthermore, you might be able to get the buyer to agree to pay you in full, early, which is called ballooning the debt. Most balloon arrangements call for early payment within three to five years of the closing, even though the loan payments are set up as if the loan is for a much longer period of time, twenty years for instance. This was the arrangement described in the Poors' case. The idea is that your buyer either will be able to refinance or sell the home on or before the due date of the balloon and pay you off. The risk of not getting paid is exemplified by what happened to the Poors.

The factor table which follows allows you to compute the monthly payments on any paper you might hold for the interest rates and loan terms shown in the table. A more complete factor table or loan amortization payment book can be obtained from most commercial lending companies.

Factor Table

Interest rate	15 years	20 years	25 years	30 years
9 %	$10.15	$ 9.00	$ 8.40	$ 8.05
9¼	10.30	9.16	8.57	8.23
9½	10.45	9.33	8.74	8.41
9¾	10.60	9.49	8.92	8.60
10	10.75	9.66	9.09	8.78
10¼	10.90	9.82	9.27	8.97
10½	11.06	9.99	9.45	9.15
10¾	11.21	10.16	9.63	9.34
11	11.37	10.33	9.81	9.53
11¼	11.53	10.50	9.99	9.72
11½	11.69	10.67	10.17	9.91
11¾	11.85	10.84	10.35	10.10
12	12.01	11.02	10.54	10.29
12¼	12.17	11.19	10.72	10.48
12½	12.33	11.37	10.91	10.68
12¾	12.49	11.54	11.10	10.87
13	12.66	11.72	11.28	11.07
13¼	12.82	11.90	11.47	11.26
13½	12.99	12.08	11.66	11.46
13¾	13.15	12.26	11.85	11.66
14	13.32	12.44	12.04	11.85
14¼	13.49	12.62	12.23	12.05

The formula for computing payments using the factor table is: .001 × the loan factor × the amount of the loan. For example, if you agree to hold paper of $50,000 at 12 percent interest for twenty years, then the loan factor from the table is 11.02 and the monthly payments will be .001 × 11.02 × $50,000 = $551.

Real estate agents, of course, like to work with sellers who are willing to hold paper because that makes it easier for the agent to sell the home. But when it comes to closing time, the agent invariably will want the commission in cash, with you (like the Poors) getting the paper. I have seen deals, however, where the agent was talked into holding paper for part of the commission, which allowed the seller to get more cash or reduced the buyer's cash requirement at closing. If you want to get your agent to agree to hold paper for part of the commission, do it before you sign the sales agreement with your buyer, when the agent will be anxious about putting the deal together. Otherwise, it will be too late. And get your agent to put it in writing, signed by the broker.

Any paper you hold should be secured by a mortgage or something else of value, such as stocks or bonds. Then, if the buyer defaults on the loan, you can go after the collateral. Your buyer should be personally liable to repay you, which usually gives you the additional option of suing the buyer instead of foreclosing. The paper should contain a stiff late payment penalty to encourage your buyer to pay you on time.

You may be able to obtain what is called "mortgage insurance," which protects your paper if your buyer defaults in payment. This type of insurance has to be arranged through a commercial lender, and it would be best to make arrangements for it before you put your home on the market.

Your paper should also require the buyer to insure the home and your interest in it as a lender against fire and other disaster losses. And it might be a good idea to require credit life insurance (decreasing term) on the buyer and the buyer's spouse, if any, payable to you up to the loan amount, if the buyer dies before the loan is paid off.

If the buyer later defaults and there is another mortgage ahead of yours (called a "senior mortgage"), you could be in for a big surprise. The senior mortgage holder may be able to foreclose and cut you off, placing you in the sad position of having to pay off the senior lender to preserve your paper.

If your buyer makes a subsequent equity sale, then there could be even more surprises. First, the sale will again trigger any alienation clause in a senior mortgage, which may jeopardize your paper. Second, you then will be placed in the position of relying on a third party you do not know to pay a senior lender and you. This can be prevented by putting an alienation clause in your paper.

For reasons to be discussed, you must state in the contract of sale what the terms of your paper will be. In fact, I feel it is best to actually draw up the loan documents before signing the final contract and attach them to it, initialed by you and the buyer. Otherwise, you could find yourself arguing with the buyer at the closing over the terms of the paper, some of which will be critical to you.

As you can see, holding paper is an area that can cause you big trouble. For that reason, you should have a good real estate lawyer at your side, before you agree to do it. I will tell you even more about how to hold paper later, but let's now turn to the commercial lenders.

Commercial lenders. Commercial lenders are firms in the business of lending people money, and they do it with the idea of making a profit. They make various types of commercial loans such as VA, FHA, Federal Land Bank, Farmers Home Administration, conventional and so forth.

Points and closing costs. Commercial lenders usually require substantial closing costs and fees, which are paid at the time of closing. The most common terms you hear are "discount" and "loan fee," each of which can run from one to several percentage points of the amount of your purchaser's loan. The discount is related to what the current interest rate is, and it can be very high. It is tax deductible, if paid by the buyer. The IRS says it isn't deductible if paid by the seller, because the seller isn't the debtor. The loan fee is charged to cover the costs of processing the loan, and can run from one to several points, depending on lenders and local practices. The IRS says the loan fee is not tax deductible, regardless of who pays it, but a lot of people take it anyway, gambling on not being audited.

On a $50,000 loan, a two-point discount and a two-point

loan fee will add $2,000 ([.02 + .02] × $50,000) to the cost of selling your home, and this will come out of your or the buyer's pocket. The easiest way to get these and other closing costs[1] paid is to add what you think they will be to the agreed selling price of your home, and you agree to pay them at closing. (Sellers have to pay the discount points on VA loans.) Your buyer will actually pay them because they are added into the price, but most of these costs will be paid over the term of the loan, making it easier for the buyer to close the deal.

Here is an example: Sales price, $62,500; loan amount, $50,000 (80 percent); two-point loan fee ($1,000) and two discount points ($1,000); and $600 in other closing costs. If the buyer pays the points and closing costs, it looks like this:

Sales price		$ 62,500
Less loan (.80 × $62,500)		– 50,000
Down payment		12,500
Plus:	Points (.04 × $50,000)	2,000
	Closing costs	+ 600
Cash required		$ 15,100

If the points and other closing costs are added to the price, it works out like this:

Original sales price		$ 62,500
Plus:	Points (.04 × $50,000)	2,000[2]
	Closing costs	+ 600
Revised sales price		$ 65,100
Less revised loan (.80 × $65,100)		– 52,080
Cash required		$ 13,020

1. Appendix D outlines what these other costs might be.

2. Those with a sharp pencil will see that the points will actually be $2,083 (.04 × $52,080). But, if you show $2,083 as the points, then that will change the revised sales price and thus the amount of the revised loan and thus the points, ad infinitum. So, the seller loses $83 in this example.

So, the cash savings to the buyer is $2,080 ($15,100 - $13,020), which could make or break the deal.[3]

Another consideration, especially with VA and FHA loans, is having to make repairs to satisfy the requirements of the buyer's lender. Usually, the seller is required to make such repairs. To handle this, add what you think the repairs might cost to the agreed price of the home, just as you would with a discount or loan fee.

You are probably wondering if adding the estimated closing costs and repairs to the selling price will cause your home to be overpriced in the eyes of the lender's appraiser. Not usually. The lender and appraiser will be familiar with this technique and will try to accommodate you—the lender because he wants to collect the points and earn the interest; the appraiser, who knows this and would like to keep the lender's business.

If you agree to pay the loan costs or make repairs required by the lender, state in the contract the most you will pay. Discounts can go up, and repairs can run more than planned. These items can also run less. Therefore, you and your buyer will probably want you to agree to adjust the price at closing if these costs turn out to be more or less than stated in the contract. Most lenders do not like to know about such agreements, which are often illegal. For that reason, these types of reimbursement agreements are made separately and not shown to the lender. This is a common practice.

Your buyer may want you to hold paper behind a new first mortgage to cover part of the buyer's down payment. This is allowed for some commercial loans and not for others, so find

3. There you go with your sharp pencil again trying to see if the buyer's lost tax deduction would affect this result. If the buyer is in the maximum bracket of 50 percent, the tax savings (not realized until the following April 15) is $500 (.50 × $1,000 discount). So, the buyer comes out at least $1,580 ahead after taxes ($2,080 - $500). The trade-off is that the buyer's mortgage is $2,080 larger and the monthly mortgage payments are slightly higher.

out ahead of time from the lender how he feels about your doing this. If you try to get around the lender's requirements on your holding paper, and the lender finds out, he can foreclose and cut you off. This risk can be eliminated by holding other collateral, say the buyer's stock or bonds, a savings account or a mortgage on other real estate of the buyer (or the buyer's parents). However, another risk that cannot be eliminated is that holding paper from the buyer might violate a federal or state law. Again, this is a good area for a lawyer's services.

* * * * *

The foregoing covers the basic types of financing and the problems that the various types of financing can cause you. There is quite a lot of different financing available in today's market, and it is constantly changing. Most real estate agents will know what is available and will steer your buyer to it. If you are not going to be using a real estate agent, then you must familiarize yourself with your local financing options, so that you can help your buyer get financing and, thus, be able to close.

Speaking of which, let's meet the Closing Agent.

4 *The Closing Agent*

Closing practices vary throughout the country, but the closing agent (in some areas called the "escrow" or "settlement" agent) usually is either a lawyer or a title insurance company representative. Sometimes it is the buyer's lender or your real estate broker. The closing agent is supposed to work on behalf of everyone involved (you, the buyer, the lender and the real estate agent) and is usually selected by the real estate agent. The closing agent does not represent you, but is supposed to be "neutral." Being neutral, the closing agent cannot take sides in a dispute, say, between you and the buyer. Nor can the closing agent negotiate for you.

The closing agent's job is to prepare all of the closing papers according to the terms of the sales contract and the lender's loan commitment, if any, and to make sure that title is in order, that the survey is clean, that all funds are collected and properly disbursed and the necessary documents recorded.

All too often, the closing agent feels allegiance to your real estate agent who sends the closing agent business on a regular basis, a fact seldom disclosed (the double agent problem again). In such cases, the closing agent is acutely sensitive to the overwhelming desire of the real estate agent to get the deal closed and the commission paid for all of the work the agent has done. (The lawyer in the Nathans' case faced this dilemma.) Therefore, you should carefully scrutinize any advice the closing agent gives you, and if you find yourself in a dispute with the buyer or agent, you had better run for help if you don't already have a representative. By representative, I mean someone whose advice will not be tainted by a conflicting hope that you will keep quiet and close, so that they will get paid.

Now let's talk a little about hiring this type of person.

5 *Your Own Representative*

Most people know about as much about selling a home as I know about flying an airplane—just enough to crash and burn. And few people are tough enough to negotiate, preferring instead to be liked. Even fewer people know how to negotiate or how to write a good contract. Yet, I see sellers day in and day out trying to sell their own homes without representation or relying on the often questionable advice of a real estate agent, who may be very good at selling, but not so good at advising.

The FTC's view. With every intention of being repetitive, let me once again remind you of the fact that very few real estate agents can be impartial when working on a contingency or co-op basis. Quoting from the staff report of the Federal Trade Commission study completed in 1981:

> Most consumers assume their brokers provide them with sound advice and represent them in key aspects of the transaction; however . . . most sellers are represented by brokers with varying interests, some of which are often inconsistent with the seller's interests. The ambiguities and conflicts in the broker's role lead to false consumer expectations of representation and to potential and real abuse of the broker's fiduciary duty. *These abuses include self-serving advice . . . violation of consumer confidences,* and others. (Emphasis added)

A lot of your tax dollars were spent on the FTC study, the results of which were not publicly released until May 1984. If you are wondering why the results were withheld for so long, you are not alone.

Real estate lawyers vs. brokers. You have two choices as an *advisor*: a real estate lawyer or a real estate broker or agent. They are the only ones who are legally and educationally qualified to give you advice about selling your home. And expect to pay them for it, rather than trying to get by with free advice from a friend. As the saying goes, "You get what you pay for"—no more, no less.

It will be difficult to find, as an advisor, a real estate broker or agent; either would much prefer to list your home for sale than advise you. And if you already have it listed for sale with another broker or agent, the one you approach for advice will more than likely be afraid of second-guessing and infuriating the other. This probably leaves you with seeking out a lawyer as your advisor. However, a good real estate lawyer can be quite helpful to you, especially in the planning stages and during the negotiations and contract writing, not to mention helping you pick a good agent to sell your home.

When to seek a lawyer's advice. If you decide to secure a lawyer, do so as soon as you have made your decision to sell. The further you are into the transaction when you make this decision, the less the lawyer will be able to help you. I am constantly amazed by clients who call saying that they have contracted to sell their home and want me to represent them. If they have already signed the contract, what more is there for me to do? For, you see, the contract of sale casts the die for the entire transaction. What follows after that is usually routine paper work that the lawyer's secretary can do.

If you find yourself needing legal help after signing the

contract of sale, then the odds will be very great that it's because you or your agent fouled up something earlier, as in the cases given in the Introduction. This is when you can pay dearly for legal advice. In other words, "an ounce of prevention is worth a pound of cure," as the Brights are now learning. And a little preventive advice shouldn't cost all that much. In fact, the money you spend will probably be repaid severalfold in savings that your lawyer will negotiate for you and problems that will be prevented.

What will it cost? It's still a good idea to know how much this lawyer will cost you. This usually depends on the amount of time the lawyer works for you and the amount of money involved, meaning the price of your home. You should be able to get either (1) a fixed fee or (2) an hourly rate including a quote for the maximum total charges. If you can't, go to another lawyer. In fact, you should shop around anyway, but don't sacrifice experience for a lower rate. An experienced lawyer charging $75 an hour or more often can work miracles compared to a $50-an-hour lawyer, and usually in a lot less time.

Finding the lawyer. How do you find this lawyer? Ask a title insurance company, your banker or another lawyer for a list of good residential real estate lawyers. When you interview those on the list, ask them which real estate companies and agents they represent, since they probably will want to refer you to one of these if you plan to use an agent. However, you will not want to use an agent that a lawyer represents, because the lawyer's loyalties will be divided between representing you and getting a longtime client paid. Furthermore, when you try to put into practice some of the things suggested, the lawyer will be very uncomfortable if you are using an agent that sends the lawyer business.

A silent partner. One last thing about hiring a lawyer—it could scare the dickens out of a buyer or agent, which is the last thing you want to do. So, if you hire a lawyer, try to keep it a secret. Use the lawyer as a silent partner, so to speak, at least until you and the buyer have reached an agreement. In areas where it is customary to use attorneys to represent you on home sales, this suggestion has no application.

* * * * *

In wrapping up this chapter, I wish to try to make it clear that I am not out to create business for lawyers. But the facts are the facts. Few lay people are knowledgeable about selling their homes, and real estate agents, for the reasons discussed, are "sellers," not "advisors." That leaves lawyers.

Part 2

Controlling the Game

By now you should have a better understanding of what will be going on when you sell your home, meaning, it's time to look at the "how to" side. Much of what follows is not information that real estate agents will want you to know. If you are using a lawyer as an advisor, it might be a good idea to give your lawyer this book to read beforehand. It will explain the approach you plan to take and why you wish not to be referred to any agents that send the lawyer business.

So, here goes.

6 *Pregame Strategy*

You usually will come out better if you begin your selling effort from a position of strength. The following suggestions will enable you to accomplish this goal.

Your reason for selling. There are many reasons for selling your home: being transferred, wanting to get into another school district, needing a larger home, wanting to move to the country, getting divorced, being unable to afford the loan payments on it and so on. Obviously, most people know why they are selling. Unfortunately, everyone else usually does, too.

The idea, in most cases, is to keep from the buyer the fact that you are in a hurry or anxious to sell. As previously mentioned, the buyer will be leery if nothing is said. So, if you are in a hurry or anxious, you will have to decide whether to let out the truth or tell a "little white lie," such as your mother-in-law is moving in with you and you need to find a larger (much larger) home. If you decide on the latter course, tell your agent the same thing. Otherwise, the truth will probably get to the buyer.

Your next home. If you are buying another home and are unfortunately like most people, you will try to find your next home before putting your present one on the market. You will go to a lot of time and trouble locating your new home without even knowing if your present one will sell. Then, when you do find your next home, you will probably make an offer to buy it that is contingent on your being able to sell your existing home within a certain period of time. Not having made a firm offer, you probably will not get many concessions from the seller in the negotiations.

Furthermore, the seller will probably insist on the right to continue trying to get a better offer than yours, and then have the right to require you to either put up or shut up. This is called a "break clause." It gives the seller the right to secure a second buyer and then break your contract if you do not go ahead and close without having sold your present home.

Faced with both a time limit on selling your present home and a break clause, you will be under double pressure to sell quickly. As a result, you probably will not get as much for your home as you should, which will compound your having agreed to pay too much for the one you are buying.

If you do not like that scenario, you might be interested in the approach of selling first, buying last. This takes away the time pressure when you are selling and puts you in a position to make a firm offer and thus be able to really bargain when you buy. The savings can be very large, because you will be negotiating from a position of strength, both when you sell and buy. The normal way of doing it leaves you negotiating from a weak position in both cases.

Now, this approach isn't for everyone. It might not work if you are already under time pressure to sell. Nor is it likely to work if you are a nervous person by nature, because of the uncertainty of not knowing where you will be living next. It may well happen that you will not be able to find a home that you like or can afford and will have to rent, possibly in an area that doesn't suit you. And don't overlook the fact that this approach will cost you your home interest deduction for tax purposes during the time that you are not a home owner. A visit to your tax advisor is recommended before you try this.

For those of you who like this alternative approach, there are some ways to reduce the uncertainty. You might try getting your buyer either to agree to delay the closing, perhaps for six months, or close and then rent back to you for that time. This will give you more breathing room. I prefer the latter way, because you have the buyer's money in hand. Then, if the buyer dies, goes bankrupt, gets a divorce or cold feet, you are protected.

If you cannot work out something with the buyer to let you stay in the home, then you might want to consider renting elsewhere for a while. Or, you might have relatives who can put you up or find a house in need of a house sitter. Either way will involve two moves or storing your possessions, but the hassle and small added cost should be more than repaid by the savings.

Tax consequences of selling at a gain. Finally, don't overlook the fact that there will be federal and state income tax consequences if you sell your home at a gain. However, the federal taxes are deferred if you buy another home of equal or greater value within two years after selling your present one. If you are fifty-five or older and have lived in your home three of the last five years, you also can deduct on your federal tax return up to $125,000 of any gain regardless of whether you buy another home. State tax laws may vary. A visit to your tax advisor early on will be a good idea in any event.

Job-related moves. If you are being transferred or have been hired by a new company and must move out of town, then there are special considerations for you.

Many companies which move employees either will purchase

the employee's home or have an agreement with an outside company to purchase it. If you are in this situation, then your home will be appraised by someone chosen by the purchasing company, and the appraised price is what you will be paid. You will be given a certain period of time within which to try to sell through ordinary channels for a better price. But, at the end of that time, you will have to decide whether or not to take the purchasing company's offer.

It has been my experience that the offer that you will get from the purchasing firm will be a little less than what you want to get. However, by taking such an offer (assuming you are unable to sell through ordinary channels), you avoid getting stuck with a home in another city or taking a real beating on its sale. Furthermore, having a guaranteed sale takes a lot of pressure off you and enables you to negotiate from a strong position with prospective buyers of your home as well as sellers of homes in your new city.

If your employer does not provide a guaranteed purchase, then you could be in a real jam. Under heavy pressure to sell, you will not be able to bargain well. Do everything you can to stall the relocation date. Even better, insist on being subsidized for having to take less because of the time pressure or for having to make mortgage payments on your home that you weren't able to sell before the move.

One other thing to consider is that when you go looking for your new home, you will be what agents call an "out-of-towner." Agents love working with out-of-towners because they are in a big hurry to find and buy a home. You might want to consider renting for a while to get the feel for your new location and allow yourself some time to shop around.

Guaranteed sale listing agreements. Some real estate firms offer plans similar to an employer guaranteed purchase plan. It usually works this way.

If you agree to list your home for sale with them, they will, for an additional fee, agree to purchase it at a predetermined price if it doesn't sell within a certain period of time. Again, you can expect the purchase price to be less than you feel your home is worth. By using such an arrangement, though, you eliminate the pressure to sell in a hurry and can successfully bargain for your next home. The disadvantages are paying an extra fee and getting less than your home is worth if it cannot be sold the regular way.

Some of these guaranteed purchase plans also provide for advancing you money against your equity. This option allows you to proceed with purchasing your next home before selling your present one. The loan is repaid when your present home is sold, either the regular way or under the guaranteed purchase plan. However, buying your next home before selling your present one will put enormous pressure on you to sell—especially in a buyer's market—and probably cost you a lot of money.

Guaranteed purchase plans historically have been offered on a local basis. However, ERA® Real Estate is now offering it through participating franchises on a national basis. I expect that other national real estate firms will soon follow suit.

Buyer's vs. seller's markets. The early 1980s have been very strong buyer's markets, while the 1970s were predominantly seller's markets. A seller's market is best for you, because homes move quickly then. A buyer's market will make it tougher for you to sell, get the price you want or avoid holding paper. You will know that you are in a buyer's market if homes are moving slowly and interest rates are high.

Once when I was being interviewed on a local radio station, a caller asked if I thought he and his wife should sell their home. After questioning him, I learned that he had no need to sell, wanting simply a change of scenery. I also learned that they didn't owe anything on their home. It was at that time a strong buyer's market, and my advice was to stand pat, because they wouldn't get what their home was worth and would probably end up holding a lot of paper. I later got several critical remarks about giving this advice from real estate agents who had been listening.

Another time, I was being interviewed by long distance telephone on a radio station in Austin, Texas. I suggested that buyers should be patient when house hunting because it was such a strong buyer's market. A woman called in and set me straight. Although it was a buyer's market in most places, it was a seller's market in Austin, which was booming and had an unemployment rate of only 3½ percent. Furthermore, housing prices were increasing at a rate of over 1 percent per month. This woman and her husband were, therefore, desperate to buy. So, local market conditions can vary from place to place and from national conditions.

The best time of year to sell. In addition to considering market conditions, you should also try to time selling your home during the most favorable selling months for your area. Generally, these are the milder months, for this is when homes and yards look and feel their best. Problems, such as air infiltration, poor insulation, big heating or air-conditioning bills and so forth, don't show up or mean as much in the mild months. And there is just something about mild weather that gets people out.

There are exceptions to the general rule, though. If you live in the southernmost areas of the country, then late fall and winter, when the "snow birds" are down, will probably be the best time to sell. If you have a water problem in certain months or your well gets low in dry months, put your home on the market when these problems do not exist. Although you may end up having to tell the buyer, hearing about these problems is never quite as bad as seeing or experiencing them.

If you are selling first, buying last, then you will have time to wait until toward the end of the selling season in your area to bargain with a discouraged seller. That is when you are likely to get the best price on your next home.

* * * * *

The foregoing considerations must be made to put you in a position to sell. Now, let's talk about getting your home (as opposed to you) ready to sell.

7 *Preparing the Product*

There are several preliminary considerations here, two of the more important ones being the condition of your home and the state of your title. You do not want to spend a lot of money at this point in time. If you could not afford to put a new roof on before, you certainly can't afford it now. But you should do some cosmetic sprucing up and make sure that your title is in order.

As to sprucing up, most real estate agents or residential appraisers should be able to advise you what to do. Basically, you want your home and yard clean and uncluttered (especially the closets, attic and basement). Also, repair or replace any visible rotten wood and do touch-up painting where needed. To check up on your title, you will need a real estate lawyer or a title insurance company. If you have an abstract of title or title insurance, then most of the title work will already be done.

Other selling tools. I suggest that you also have a survey at this point in time. If you cannot find your old one, then your lender or the title insurance company insuring your home should have one in their files. If not, get one made. Any smart buyer will require one, and you will want to know first if there are any problems with your property that would be disclosed by a survey, so that you can get them resolved and not risk losing a sale or getting sued when such problems surface later.

Another thing I like to see is a solid inspection report on the structural integrity of your home, the operation of its systems and appliances and wood damage (termites, beetles, borers, ants or dry rot). There should be home inspection firms in your area that offer these services at a reasonable cost.

If your home is energy efficient, you should also gather up your previous twelve months' utility bills, which a sharp buyer will want to see anyway.

There are real estate firms which offer long term buyer protection plans (warranties) on homes at a reasonable cost. These plans offer reimbursement for such things as defective wiring, plumbing, septic tanks, appliances and, sometimes, structural problems. Most home warranty companies will inspect your home before agreeing to provide coverage. The cost can be added to the selling price or paid by the buyer separately. Or, you can pay it—this is negotiable.

If you have an assumable mortgage, obtain a statement from your lender setting forth its requirements on an equity sale. Do this even if the interest rate will escalate. The last thing you want is to enter into an agreement to sell your equity, then find out you can't or that it's going to cost the buyer more than what has been agreed.

Using these to market your home. You can then present these things to prospective buyers when they visit your home. The fact that your title is in order, the survey is clean and the home has no serious problems, is energy efficient, will be covered by a warranty and has an assumable mortgage can have a very disarming effect on a buyer and strengthen your bargaining position a great deal. These precautions can also reduce the possibility of being sued by the buyer for fraud after the closing by getting the problems out on the table before anything is signed.

Using an appraisal. Another good technique is to have your home appraised by a qualified residential appraiser. If you do this, don't tell anyone so that you can use the appraisal deep in the negotiations to move the buyer closer to what you want to get. This assumes, of course, that the appraisal is favorable. If it isn't, the last thing you want is for a buyer or real estate agent to know about it.

You can also give the favorable appraisal to the buyer to be given to a commercial lender from which the buyer plans to borrow. This will save the buyer the cost of lender's appraisal, if the lender accepts yours.

Buy-downs. If you are desperate to sell and do not want to hold paper, consider making advance arrangements with a commercial lender to let you pay extra points (which come out of your sales proceeds) to "buy-down" the interest rate on any loan the lender makes to your future buyer. Buy-downs of this type will reduce the monthly mortgage payments during the early years of the buyer's loan, making the payments more affordable and your home more saleable. You also may be able to add the cost of the buy-down to the selling price, meaning you will get it back at closing. This is similar to agreeing to finance the buyer's closing costs.

Paying off your present mortgage. If you think that you will be paying off your present mortgage, now is the time to find out if you have a prepayment penalty. If so, can you get it waived, or can you get the loan discounted when you pay it off? Knowing the answers to these questions will affect how much you will ask for your home.

* * * * *

Now you have your home ready to sell. The next question is, what price should you ask for it.

8 *Asking and Taking Prices*

Wanting and getting your price are two different things. Most people like to bargain, so you should ask more than you plan to take. How much more is hard to say for a particular case, but about 5 to 10 percent is a general rule of thumb.[1] Applying that to an example, if you want to get $75,000, ask between $78,750 ($75,000 + .05 × $75,000) and $82,500 ($75,000 + .10 × $75,000).

Proud sellers. You also need to know if your asking and taking prices are reasonable. If you are like most sellers, then you will think that your home is worth more than it is. When I work with sellers, I try to get them to tell me how much they would pay for their home if they were going to buy it. Their first response is invariably a figure representing what they want to get for it. It takes a while, but I eventually get them to look at it from the other side, and then the figure comes down, often substantially. After bringing them down to earth, I then try to price their home using facts, not emotions.

Determining value. The main consideration is the selling price of similar homes in your area and neighborhood, not

1. Statistics, for the city in which I live, indicate that homes sold for an average of 94 percent of their list (asking) price.

their asking prices. You arrive at a taking price based on comparable sales, then add, say, 10 percent to that to get your asking price. Any real estate agent or appraiser can get the comparables, to which you should give great weight. Agents do this free of charge prior to listing your home for sale, which gives you the option of using an agent's appraisal without committing to give the agent the listing. Therefore, you should be able to get several agents' appraisals, which will give you a better idea of what to ask than a single agent will give you. If you will be selling it yourself, you might want to use an appraiser, whose fee should be in the $150–$300 range, possibly more, depending on locale and the value of your home.

Drawbacks to appraisals. Some warnings about both types of appraisals are in order at this point. Agents often will understate a home's true value to get it sold quickly. For example, if your home is worth $80,000, but your agent talks you into selling it for $70,000, the agent and broker, working on a 6 percent commission, get $4,200. The extra effort that would be required to get you $80,000 would only return them an additional $600 (.06 × [$80,000 - $70,000]). Rather than making the extra effort, many agents would rather sell another $80,000 home for $70,000 and get another $4,200, not $600. If the sales commission is co-oped with another agent or firm, then the incentive to get you the extra $10,000 would be even less.

The opposite problem often occurs, too. Here, an agent, in order to get your listing, will give you a high appraisal in line with your biased view of the value of your home. Then the agent will wait for you to reduce your asking price. By then, your home probably will be shop worn and will bring less than its real value.

How will you know if your agent is leveling with you about the value of your home? One way to test the agent is to act like you want more than you know the home is worth (assuming you know its worth). If the agent argues that you are too high, then you are not dealing with the second type of agent described. If the agent refuses the listing, then you know that you are not dealing with the first type either. At this point, you concede that the agent is correct and enter into a listing agreement.

The best way I know to be prepared to discuss your listing price with an agent is to have your home appraised before meeting with the agent. However, be careful not to do something that would distort the appraiser's judgment of the value of your home. I have seen many cases where the seller followed the appraiser through every room, into the basement and attic and out into the yard, extolling the home's special qualities. The result was an appraisal more in line with the owner's feelings than reality. The MAI[2] professional designation that you see after many appraiser's names has often been said to stand for "Made As Instructed."

Doing your own appraisal. You can also do your own appraisal by visiting the homes in your area that are for sale or have recently sold. The inside condition of a home can have a positive or negative impact on price. So, just because a three bedroom, two bath, split-level down the street sold for or is priced at $75,000 doesn't mean that yours of similar description will either bring that or should be priced at that figure. In other words, go inside.

The size of your home relative to neighboring homes is important, too. If you home is larger than the other homes, they will tend to lower its value. If, on the other hand, it is smaller than surrounding homes, they will tend to increase its value.

2. Member of the Appraisal Institute.

Other factors affecting your price. The price you can expect to ask and get will also be affected by other factors: paying a real estate commission, having a prepayment penalty, having a mortgage assumable at a favorable interest rate, your ability to hold paper at a favorable interest rate, whether it's a buyer's or seller's market, whether you are selling from a strong or weak position and so forth.

* * * * *

The more patient you can be about selling your home and the easier you can make it for a buyer to pay for it, the more you can ask and expect to get. But don't be greedy. If you ask too much in hopes that someone will come along and pay it, you will turn off agents and buyers, and your home could end up shop worn. When that happens, agents and buyers quit coming to see it, and you end up taking a real beating.

9 *For Sale By Owner?*

If you think that selling your home yourself will *save* you money, think again. You will have to *earn* any commission that you are trying to save, and you may well end up with a lot less than you would have gotten using an agent.

Why you should not try it. Agents have access to buyers and MLS, and you don't. Furthermore, agents are trained in selling homes, and you aren't. Day in and day out, they will beat your results, even after you pay the commission. Furthermore, they will save you a lot of trouble.

For instance, if you sell your home yourself, you will have to be around to take the phone calls that your ads will produce, and you will have to be ready to show when a prospective buyer is ready to see, which is usually when the buyer calls, not next Wednesday night. Agents are also good at helping buyers get financing, which you probably won't be. Furthermore, when you put your home on the market, For Sale By Owner, agents will call you and worry you to death for a listing. Another thing an agent can do that you won't be in a position to do is to screen buyers to make sure that they are bona fide and not burglars casing your home. Finally, if you try to sell yourself, then turn it over to an agent after nothing happens, your home will be shop worn and the agent will want to lower the asking price.

If you still want to do it. For you diehards, here are some suggestions that might help you sell your home yourself. First, get with a good real estate lawyer and familiarize yourself with whatever financing is available. Next, obtain some form sales contracts so that you will be ready to sign up a willing buyer on the spot. Then, write a newspaper ad describing your home and noting in conspicuous letters that it is FOR SALE BY OWNER. Look at ads being run by the agents to get an idea of what information needs to be in an ad. End the ad with these words, prominently displayed: AGENTS WELCOME. Put those magic words on the sign you put out in the front yard, too, for they tell agents that you will pay them a half commission for bringing you a buyer. Don't be too proud to work with an agent on this basis. Finally, get a telephone recorder to take down the calls that will come in when you are out.

In many areas, there are firms which offer For Sale By Owner multiple listing services. In my area, there are two such firms: one uses a local cable television channel, and the other uses a magazine which is distributed through local convenience, drug and grocery stores. I suspect that a service of this type will soon be offered through some sort of centralized computer terminal with a telephone tie-in.

If any of these services are available in your area, consider using them. The more exposure your home gets, the more traffic you will have and the better your selling odds will be.

Buyer reaction. You will find, I believe, that most buyers will expect a discount on the price because you aren't using an agent. Offer to split the difference with them. For instance, if your home is on the market for $100,000 and an agent would charge 6 percent, offer to reduce the asking price by half of what the agent would have gotten, or $3,000. This saves money for both you and the buyer. But understand that most buyers will consider $97,000 your asking, not taking, price when you do this, and the buyer's first offer probably will be for a lot less. If you have done what I suggested and have marked up the asking price about 5 to 10 percent over what you are willing to take, then you will have room to negotiate, even after knocking $3,000 off the price.

Another problem I have seen is that buyers are often leery of homes being sold by the owner. They feel that the owner is not using an agent because there is something wrong with the home that the owner is trying to hide. The suggestions made in Chapter 7 should take care of this buyer concern.

So, if you have the time and thick skin, try it.

10 *Working with an Agent*

As much as I criticize the real estate system, I still believe, for the reasons stated in the preceding chapter, that you will come out better hiring an agent to sell your home.

Which agent? I strongly caution against using a friend or relative. They know your affairs which you don't want passed on to prospective buyers—you are being transferred, just got divorced, have agreed to buy another home, etc. Or, if your relative or friend messes something up, how do you end the relationship gracefully? And can you take advice from a friend or relative without getting your feelings hurt? Or, will a friend or relative be afraid to be frank with you? Get an agent you aren't emotionally tied to.

The type of agent you will want will be someone who knows and sells a lot of homes in your neighborhood or area and who is a full-time, not part-time, agent. This information can be obtained from a real estate lawyer, title insurance company or your banker. And look at the agent's firm. You will want one that uses MLS so that your home will have maximum exposure to buyers. If an agent tries to talk you out of listing in MLS, look out. That agent is trying to hog the commission and your home will not get the exposure it needs. The only exception to this is when the agent already has a buyer lined up to make an offer.

Another thing about real estate firms is that most teach their agents to show their own firm's listings ahead of those of other firms. A real estate firm makes more money on listings its agents sell, because it does not have to co-op the commission with another firm. For this reason, you will probably want to use an agent who works for one of the larger real estate firms. The larger the firm, the more agents it will have to show buyers your home.

The listing agreement. After you pick an agent, you will be asked to sign a listing agreement. This is a legally binding contract that will give your agent's firm the exclusive right to sell your home. This means that the agreed commission will be due the agent's firm regardless of who finds the buyer, even if it's you. This is standard, and you should agree to it. Why make the agent mad? Besides, this is the only kind of agreement that MLS will accept in most areas. The one exception to this is when your employer offers you a guaranteed purchase if you cannot sell through ordinary channels. In this case, you will be able to get a sale to the purchasing company excluded from the listing agreement.

The agent will probably want a ninety-day or longer listing. Agree to it. Most listing agreements are voidable anytime at the will of the seller, which the agent knows but probably will not tell you. The only thing that you can't do is cancel the listing and deal directly with a prospective buyer, who has been put on the property or produced by the agent or the agent's ads or sign. If you do, you will still owe a commission and may even be liable to the agent for fraud.

I have often seen sellers tell an agent, "I don't care what you make on the deal as long as I get my price." This type of arrangement is called a "net listing" and is illegal. The agent's commission has to be set by some ascertainable standard, either as a percentage of the selling price, a flat fee, an hourly rate or a combination of these arrangements. In practically every case, the commission will be a straight percentage, ranging between 6 and 7 percent in most areas. If it's for less than that, you will be risking other agents steering their buyers elsewhere. For this reason, I advise against using discount brokers, whose low fees appear so attractive. Traditional agents and brokers tend to avoid showing a discount broker's listings, to discourage discounting.

Negotiating the commission. Negotiating commissions is something that agents hate to do, but the law requires that commissions be negotiable. Nevertheless, most real estate firms have policies about what their commissions will be, and if you try to negotiate the commission at the outset, you will get a lot of resistance. Furthermore, the commission you agree to pay is published in MLS, meaning all other agents with potential buyers for your home know what commission you will pay. If other agents feel that the commission you are paying is too low, they will, as mentioned above, steer their buyers away from your home.

For these reasons, the time to negotiate the commission or ask the agent to hold paper for part of the commission is when you get an offer below your asking price or which does not cash you out (i.e., where you have to hold paper instead of getting paid now). An agent is not automatically entitled to a commission, unless the offer is for your full asking (the list) price and terms from a buyer ready, willing and able to close. So, if the offer is for less, you can renegotiate the commission. This deep into the transaction, your agent will have invested a lot of time and effort in the deal and will probably already have mentally spent the commission. When the commission arrangement is altered at this point in time, the new arrangement doesn't get put in MLS, so your agent and firm won't lose face before their peers.

If you intend to negotiate the commission this way, do it just before you reach an agreement with the buyer, when the agent will be the most anxious about the deal working out. For instance, if the buyer has worked up to an offer of $73,000 and your taking price is $75,000, tell the agent you will split the difference. Then give the agent some time to go off and sulk—and think. Get the new arrangement in writing from the agent's *broker*. The agent has no legal authority to bind the broker or real estate firm to the new commission agreement.

The fewer agents and real estate firms involved, the more commission reduction you should be able to achieve. For instance, if your agent also finds the buyer, the agent and broker will get the listing and co-op commission, whereas they would have only gotten the listing commission (one-half of the total commission) if another firm's agent furnished the buyer. You may be able to get a sizeable commission reduction in such cases. However, if there are two agents involved, and one or two firms, point out that anything that they give up will be divided three or four ways, and won't affect their commissions that much. Mention how much you have lowered the asking price and offer to lower it a little more *if* they will reduce the commission and get the buyer to move a little more. I use this approach often and with good success.

Agents act very offended when asked to cut their commissions or hold paper, and they are skilled at making you feel horrible for even suggesting it. But they don't think a thing about asking you to drop the price (like The Accountant's Father) or hold paper (like the Poors) to make a deal. So don't feel too sorry for them.

If your home doesn't sell. What if your agent isn't getting results? You will need to meet and hear what the agent has to say. It may be that there is something about your home that nobody thought about that is turning buyers off, such as you are on too busy a street. It could also be the financing that is or is not available. But if your agent says that the home is simply overpriced, then you've probably been had.

If the home is overpriced, the agent almost certainly knew that it was but went along with you to get the listing, knowing that you would later swallow your pride and come down on the price. In other words, the agent wasn't straight with you when you negotiated the listing, and you should consider switching agents. This won't get you any more money for your home, but it will get you away from this type of person.

Whatever you do, though, if you suspect a problem, act on it quickly. You don't want whatever it is to keep your home from selling and cause it to become shop worn. If that happens and you then change agents, the new agent will want a substantial reduction in the asking price. Why attempt on a contingency basis what another agent couldn't do?

If you are buying and selling. If you are going to buy another home, should you use the same agent for both deals? Perhaps. On one hand, the agent will tend to work a lot harder for you with two commissions riding on the outcome; it's also easier to get an agent to negotiate the commission in such cases. You have more to offer—two deals instead of one. On the other hand, the agent normally will owe you a fiduciary duty only as the listing agent. When you start looking for your next home, the agent will then be working as a co-op agent—the agent, in other words, of your potential seller. So, in the purchase of your next home, "your" agent will owe the seller, not you, a fiduciary duty and will be legally required to get that seller, at your expense, the best possible deal. If you have any secrets you do not wish to be disclosed to your seller, or if you expect "your" agent to really negotiate for you on your next home, well, dream on.

There is a way to have it both ways, though. Tell your

agent that, as a condition of getting both deals, he or she will have to work as a buyer-paid agent on the home you will be buying—not as a co-op agent. In other words, you will pay two commissions, one on the sale of your home, the other on the purchase of your next home. This will cause the agent to owe you a fiduciary duty on both deals. If you are lucky, the agent will be familiar with being paid by a buyer. More than likely, though, the agent will go into shock. As a general rule, agents do not like being paid by the buyer, but there's nothing illegal about it, as long as they aren't paid by the seller, too. Here's how it works.

Suppose you are selling a $100,000 home and buying one in the $150,000 range. You probably will enter into a listing agreement on your present home providing for a 6 to 7 percent sales commission. As previously discussed, you may or may not wish to negotiate the listing commission at this point in time. At the same time, you enter into a *buyer-paid* listing agreement for your next home. In this agreement, you agree to pay the agent a commission on the closing of your next home. Most agents that accept buyer-paid listings will ask for one-half of a commission (3 to 3½ percent of the purchase price). Some require a retainer, perhaps $1,000, to defray expenses and bind you to them. Some will want a flat fee, perhaps $5,000, and argue that this is the best arrangement for you. Why? Because, they will say, working on a percentage penalizes them for getting you a better deal.

Remember the agents who try to list a home for less than it's worth, to sell it quickly and move on to another deal? The same psychology applies here. Furthermore, the true conflict, as discussed earlier, has nothing to do with percentage commissions. An agent working on a contingency basis—no closing, no commission—is what really can cause you problems. So don't agree to a flat fee arrangement, unless it's likely to cost less than a percentage deal.

I feel that you will come out better by getting the agent to agree to an hourly rate, for instance $75 per hour, with a limit on the total fee of $5,000 on a $150,000 home. This gives you the chance to save money, if a quick purchase is made, while limiting your exposure. However, if you decide not to buy, then you have spent your money for nothing. So, don't agree to an hourly fee arrangement, unless you are sure that you will complete the purchase of your next home.

Another thing to consider is the possibility that you may find a home on your own without your agent's help. Most buyer-paid listing agreements provide that you will owe the commission when you buy, regardless of who finds the home—even if it's you. However, your ability to offer two deals should give you the bargaining power to get the agent to exclude from the buyer-paid listing agreement any homes that you find on your own.

Another aspect of a buyer-paid listing that needs to be explained is the amount of the commission that your seller will pay (assuming the seller is using an agent). You certainly don't want to pay your agent and have the seller's agent get a full commission at the closing. That puts an extra commission into the cost of the home. You avoid this by getting your agent to talk with the listing agent and seller—*before you make an offer*—about reducing the seller's commission by one-half and the *sales* price by like amount. Your agent should get this in writing, in case the listing agent or seller conveniently forget the agreement. Only after having this agreement do you make an offer. Believe it or not, this works out dollar-wise the same as the traditional way. Let's look at an example.

Suppose you agree to pay your buyer-paid agent a 3½ percent commission. Suppose further that your buyer-paid agent negotiates the sales price down to $150,000 from $170,000, thus saving you $20,000. (Note, your agent could not legally do this as a co-op agent working for the seller, and the final sales price probably would have been higher.) Here's how the numbers would look:

Traditional Way

Sales price	$ 150,000
Less commission (.07 × $150,000)	– 10,500
Net to seller	$ 139,500

New Way

Sales price	$ 150,000
Less co-op commission (.035 × $150,000)	– 5,250
Adjusted sales price	$144,750
Less listing commission (.035 × $150,000)	– 5,250
Net to seller	$ 139,500

You can see from this example that on a $150,000 sales price, the result either way of doing it is:

Cost to you	$150,000
Net to seller	$139,500
Each agent gets	$5,250

The difference in the two approaches is that you do not have an agent doing it the traditional way and you do the new way.

An alternative, which is preferred by some buyer-paid agents, is to let your agent be paid by the seller as usual, but write into the contract the following:

> The co-op agent represents the Buyer, not the Seller, but shall be paid by Seller solely for the Buyer's convenience.

This is legal, as long as the seller agrees to it, and the seller will if explained how a co-op agent working the regular way can create legal liability for the seller to the buyer. If the co-op commission to be paid your agent will exceed what you have agreed to pay, get your agent to give you the overage.

One final thing about buyer-paid agents. If the one you are working with tries to show you a home that she or another agent in her firm has listed, then there will be a conflict of interest. Both you and the seller will be represented by the same agent or firm, as the case may be. If this happens, an election will have to be made by the agent(s) to drop either you or the seller. This could get pretty confusing, and the best solution might be to just not look at homes listed by your agent or her firm.

If you have trouble locating a buyer-paid agent, write or call Who's Who in Creative Real Estate, 921 E. Main St., Suite F, Ventura, CA, 93001, (805) 643-2337; or James B. Warkentin, 6641 Backlick Rd., Suite 201, Springfield, VA, 22150, (703) 451-6166. Either will have information about buyer-paid agents in your area. If there are not any, you can create one by dangling two deals before a traditional agent. Be patient; it will happen.

*   *   *   *   *

So much for agents. Let's turn now to the nitty-gritty—making a deal with a buyer.

11 The Contract Negotiations

Your marketing plan eventually will bring you an offer from a prospective buyer and the contract negotiations will begin. This is where the going can really get tough.

The offer. You will be made what is called an "offer" by a prospective buyer. This should always be in writing, and is usually made on a fill-in-the-blanks form contract put out by a local title insurance company or real estate firm. The offer will most likely be for less than you are asking—maybe a lot less. Don't get mad if it is. Most buyers have a higher paying price than their offering price, just like you will have a lower taking price than your asking price. The idea is to end up somewhere in the middle—hopefully above your taking price.

Sellers often get mad at agents for bringing them a low offer. To me, a low offer is better than no offer at all, and the buyer may be prepared to go much higher. You will find out soon enough, after you get into the negotiations, whether the buyer is trying to steal your home or is just testing you before making a serious offer. Another thing to remember is that agents are required by law (and Realtors® by their Code of Ethics) to present you with any offer that has been made, even if instructed by you not to present one below a certain price.

Researching the buyer. The first thing that you should do after receiving an offer is to find out everything that you can about the buyer. If you aren't using an agent, then you will have to sit down with the buyer and slyly extract this information yourself. If you are using an agent, he or she will be the best source of this information. If there is a co-op agent, then this is the person who will have the information you need.

Having worked closely with the buyer, the co-op agent probably will be reluctant to disclose the buyer's situation to you. So be prepared to remind the agent about fiduciary duty and who is paying the commission.[1] If this doesn't do the trick, suggest that the agent work out a commission arrangement with the buyer because that is the person the agent has chosen to represent. As you might imagine, the agent will be mighty uncomfortable by now and should start talking. But, if this doesn't work either, suggest filing a complaint against the agent with your local Board of Realtors® and Real Estate Commission.[2] Firmness will get the information you need.

The information you are seeking will be such things as the following: how much cash the buyer has to make the purchase; the maximum mortgage payments the buyer can afford; whether the buyer has another home to sell and how that sale is going; whether the buyer is under time pressure or whether the buyer is interested in another home. Knowing such things is crucial to being able to negotiate with a buyer.

1. In this regard *Standard of Practice 22-1* of the National Association of Realtors® interprets NAR's Code of Ethics as follows:

> It is the obligation of the selling broker as subagent of the listing broker to disclose immediately all pertinent facts to the listing broker prior to as well as after the contract is executed.

2. Appendix E contains a sample grievance complaint form for filing with your local Board of Realtors® or state real estate regulatory agency. Appendix A contains a listing for each state's regulatory agency.

Should you negotiate face-to-face? If you are using an agent, you and the buyer will probably be kept apart during the negotiations. Agents do this for a variety of reasons. They do not feel that sellers can negotiate; they feel that sellers say things that scare buyers away and they fear that the seller and buyer will scheme to cut out the agent or reduce the commission. There is a lot of truth here. Nevertheless, there's no good reason why you can't sit down face-to-face with a buyer if you want to. If you are tough inside, you will probably come out better, because you will be able to personally evaluate the buyer when the pressure is on instead of relying on an agent who is either a poor negotiator or reluctant to negotiate tough for fear of killing the deal. If you aren't tough inside, let your agent handle it.

Counteroffers. In any event, you are now ready to make what is called a "counteroffer." All offers made by you or the buyer after the buyer's initial offer are considered new offers, but they are called counteroffers. Before making your first counteroffer, review the buyer's situation. The more rushed the buyer is, the higher your taking price should be. So, you may want to mentally raise your taking price, if the facts are favorable for doing this, before deciding what your counteroffer will be.

If you are being asked by the buyer to hold paper, you should mentally raise your taking price a lot. If the terms initially offered do not include a balloon payment, then you should mentally raise your taking price even further. In fact, you might want your taking price to be your asking price or even more than that. The reason for this is that you will probably be asked to give the buyer a lower than market rate of interest. So, if you lower the price, too, you will lose out two ways—price and interest return. You can offset the loss in interest with a higher price.

Normally, though, your first counteroffer to the buyer will be for less than your asking price and terms. How much less? Well, that depends on your buyer. If your buyer is anxious to buy, you can afford to be patient—come down slowly in other words. You should also take the waiting game approach if your buyer's first offer is too low. Otherwise, you will give the buyer the impression that you are anxious—even if you aren't. Once the buyer gets that impression about you, it will be difficult to get a decent offer. If, on the other hand, the buyer makes a reasonable first offer, one close to your taking price, then you will want to move a little faster. This buyer is serious and probably a quick negotiator—one who doesn't like playing around. If you play hard-to-get with this type of buyer, it probably will kill the negotiations.

Although it is walking a fine line, I find that it usually works out best, especially in a seller's market or when you have an anxious buyer, if you do not at first accept what has been offered, even if it is your taking price or terms. Try, instead, to get the buyer to accept your counteroffer. For example, suppose a buyer has offered $72,000 and your taking price is $74,000. You counter $76,000. If the buyer then counters $74,000 and you take it, then you have lost the chance to get the buyer to pay $75,000. So, counteroffer $75,000 or $75,250. You are the only one (I hope) who knows that you will take the buyer's last counteroffer, and the buyer probably will make another and higher counteroffer. If not, then you can accept the $74,000 offer, assuming that it hasn't been retracted, which is the risk you face negotiating this way. You can negotiate the amount of paper you will hold, the interest rate, the term of the loan and length of the balloon in this fashion, too.

If you had an appraisal done by a qualified residential appraiser and it is higher than the buyer's offer, now is the time to show it to the buyer. This is also a good time to suggest to your agent that, for you to accept the offer, the agent will have to knock $1,000 off the commission. It's just like playing poker—the next move is up to the buyer and agent.

* * * * *

The foregoing covers the basics of your contract negotiations. In the next four chapters, we will look at some specific areas that could cause you a lot of trouble if you do not negotiate carefully.

12 *Should You Hold Paper?*

Although discussed previously, this is such a critical area for you that further explanation is in order. In a buyer's market, you may have no choice but to hold paper to sell your home. In a seller's market, you can usually avoid having to hold paper, because your buyer will be able to afford the financing that is being offered in the market place.

How it works. In most cases, holding paper goes hand-in-hand with an equity sale. Using a simple example, suppose your home is worth $100,000 and has a $50,000 first mortgage (called a "first" or "senior mortgage") against it that can be passed on to your buyer. Assume further no closing costs or real estate commission. You could insist on the entire $50,000 equity being paid in cash; you could hold paper (called a "second") for $50,000 or take $25,000 in cash and a $25,000 second.[1]

If you need all $50,000 to buy another home, then the last alternative won't work for you, unless you can get your seller to take $25,000 in paper, too. But if you only need $25,000 in cash, then you can live with this arrangement, regardless of

1. If there were two senior mortgages ahead of you, then your paper would be a "third." There's no limit on the number of senior mortgages that can be ahead of you. I have seen as many as five. In such a case, your paper would be a "sixth."

what happens on the other end. And, if you put a balloon payment in the paper, say, three years out, then you won't have your money tied up for very long. This assumes, of course, that your buyer will be able to come up with the balloon payment when it falls due. (Remember the Poors.)

Protective steps. Therefore, it will be very important before agreeing to hold paper to do a good credit check on the buyer. At the very least, make the deal contingent on the buyer furnishing, to your satisfaction within a certain number of days, a financial statement, an employment history to determine job stability, and a letter from the buyer's employer confirming the buyer's employment and level of compensation. Some buyers will balk at this, but if they do, just say that any commercial lender would require at least this and that your requirements are, therefore, reasonable. Check out the information the buyer gives you, just in case the buyer is dishonest.

The last thing you want is for your buyer to default and put you into a position of having to foreclose or sue on the debt to collect what you are owed. Furthermore, any senior mortgage holder may be able to foreclose, too, and cut you off. Or, a senior mortgage holder may already be foreclosing because the buyer defaulted on the senior mortgage as well. In either event, you will probably have to start making payments on the senior mortgage to keep it out of foreclosure.

Because of these risks, a credit check may not be enough to protect you. You should get the holder of any senior mortgage to agree to give you written notice of nonpayment or other default. It will also be a very good idea to get as much *cash* as possible from your buyer, as this will provide the buyer with a strong incentive to pay the senior mortgage and your second as they fall due. This will also give you a cushion to fall back on if your buyer later defaults. Small down payment arrangements are very dangerous for a seller because they give the buyer little, if any, incentive to stick it out when the going gets rough.

As mentioned in Chapter 3, you should also insist on the buyer being personally liable on the senior mortgage(s) and your second. This gives you the choice (in most states) of either foreclosing or suing the buyer on the debt if there is a default, which gives the buyer an additional incentive to pay the senior mortgage(s) and your second. Also, provide in your paper that a default in the senior mortgage(s) is a default on your second. Then you can foreclose, if a senior mortgage isn't paid, regardless of what is happening on your second. Try to arrange to have mortgage and credit life insurance, which will pay you off if your buyer quits paying or dies. Finally, require that the buyer furnish you with a hazard insurance policy insuring you against destruction or damage to the house by fire, storm and other disasters.

Wraparounds. An alternative way of holding paper in our example is to take back what is called a "wraparound" or "all-inclusive" mortgage. This would also be a second but is set up a little differently. Let's figure one on your $100,000 home with a $50,000 first.[2]

Instead of taking back a $25,000 second and $25,000 cash, with the buyer taking over the payments on the senior mortgage, you take a $75,000 wraparound and $25,000 in cash. You keep paying the senior mortgage and pocket the difference between the payments on the wraparound and the first. Both ways, you are taking back a second and loaning the buyer $25,000, but the wraparound can be better for you.

Since you are making the payments on the senior mortgage, you will always know if it's current. With a straight second, you may not find out about the first being in default until it is

2. Wraparounds are often used when there is more than one senior mortgage. The example assumes there is only one senior mortgage.

way in arrears. Another attractive feature to a wraparound is that it can increase your rate of return on the money you are loaning your buyer. For instance, assume that the interest rate on your first is 9 percent and that the interest rate you will charge your buyer is 11 percent. With a straight second, you make 11 percent on your $25,000 loan. With the wraparound, you make that plus 2 percent on the amount of the first. (You collect 11 percent on the wraparound and pay 9 percent on the first, netting you 2 percent on the first.)

Before you decide to take back a wraparound to get that extra return, there are some more things you should know about wraparounds. First, they do not work very well when the interest rate or payments on the senior mortgage(s) are higher than what you can get on the wraparound, because the spread is then negative. Second, a wraparound does not work well when there is an alienation clause in a senior mortgage, because the spread is usually eliminated when you sell by an increase in the interest rate of the senior mortgage (assuming it isn't due-on-sale and called outright). Furthermore, if your buyer later sells the home, this will again trigger any alienation clause in a senior mortgage, requiring you to have to go beg its holder for mercy. So, if a senior mortgage has an alienation clause, insist on having one just like it in your wraparound, which will give you some measure of protection on a later equity sale.

You can also use a balloon payment with wraparounds. If you do, make the balloon for the full amount of the wraparound. Then, when it is paid, you will pay off all senior mortgages and no longer be responsible for them. The suggestions given for screening buyers with poor credit and protecting yourself against default, the buyer dying or a hazard loss apply equally to wraparounds.

Holding paper and title. There are also some interesting ways to hold paper while retaining title until the full purchase price has been paid. These arrangements are called by various names: bonds for title, contracts for deed, lease/sale contracts, land sales contracts and so on. Except for the fact that you retain title, these transactions look like second or wraparound mortgages. However, the buyer's payments are treated as *rent* until you have been paid in full. The advantage to you of these arrangements is that you do not (in most states) have to foreclose to get the property back when the buyer defaults. Rather, the buyer is considered a mere tenant and can be evicted for nonpayment of rents like any other tenant. The disadvantages are similar to taking back a mortgage, plus one more—your buyer usually can walk away from the deal and you can't do anything about it. Even so, this will be the best arrangement for you in a little or no money down deal.

The relationship of price to interest rate. As previously mentioned, you probably will be asked to hold paper at a below market rate of interest. This has the effect of reducing the price you will get for your home, often a lot more than you might suspect or be told by a real estate agent.

For instance, assume the agreed price is $70,000 with a $10,000 down payment and $60,000 in paper to be held by you for twenty years. Assume further that market interest rates are 13 percent and you are to give your buyer 11 percent. Obviously, your 11 percent paper isn't worth $60,000, if you could invest $60,000 at 13 percent.

If you were to go out and buy a $60,000, 11 percent corporate or government bond due in twenty years when interest rates were 13 percent, you would be able to get it at a discounted price, perhaps $53,000. The main factors affecting the amount of the discount would be: the safety of the bond; market interest rates; how many years are left on the bond and the expected direction of market interest rates and inflation. The safer the bond, the smaller the spread between the bond rate and market interest rates, the shorter the term, and/or the better the outlook for falling interest rates and inflation, the smaller the discount would tend to be.

Your paper is just like a bond, only it is secured by a home, not the balance sheet of some corporation or government. So, you could expect a similar discount of around $7,000, making your paper worth only $53,000 and your real selling price $63,000 ($53,000 + the $10,000 down payment). If the bond or your paper had a five-year balloon in it, the term would be shortened and the discount reduced, say, to $2,000 making the bond or your paper worth $58,000 and your real sales price $68,000 ($58,000 + $10,000).

Regardless of whether you have a balloon, you can see that you would have to charge more than $70,000 to realize that much. Most lenders and real estate departments of banks can make the computation, which is quite complex, or you can just guesstimate it.

Selling your paper. You will really get your eyes opened if you try to sell your paper. Most commercial lenders and several local real estate firms in your area will dicker with you for your paper, if it meets their guidelines. The main guidelines are commercially acceptable documents (which a lawyer should prepare), a home in good condition, and a low loan-to-value ratio. In the example given, the loan-to-value ratio is 86 percent ($60,000 2 $70,000). Anything above 80 percent is probably too high, and it would be better to keep it below 60 percent, if you plan to sell your paper.

I canvassed three firms that buy seller-held paper and asked them what they would pay for this $60,000 second mortgage. Disregarding the high loan-to-value ratio, one said it would pay $52,932 less two discount points, another offered $50,769, and the third offered $39,984. Each had its own formula for making the computations, the results of which were uniformly bad for the owner of the paper.

I asked them what they would pay if the paper contained a five-year balloon, and each said that would improve the offer by an amount that would have to be negotiated. So, it would pay to shop around, before you agree to hold paper, to find out what you will end up getting for it.

The foregoing illustrates why holding paper is a trap for the unwary and why real estate agents want you, not them, to hold it. If you will have to hold paper, insist on a short balloon (five years or less) and pray that interest rates go down and that your buyer can come up with the money by the balloon date.

The "Imputed Interest" rule. The Internal Revenue Service (IRS) has an old rule that also is a trap for the unwary seller holding paper. Basically, the rule says that, if you do not charge a certain amount of interest on your paper, you will be treated as if you are charging a higher rate. This will have the effect of changing part of the payments you are to receive from principal to interest, which will be horrible for you.

The *principal* (the amount owed), on one hand, is either not taxable or is taxed in part as a capital gain, depending on whether or not you sold at a gain. If you buy another home of equal or greater cost within two years, the capital gain is deferred. If you are over 55, then up to $125,000 of your capital gain is permanently excluded from you income. The *interest*, on the other hand, is not deferred or excluded and is usually taxed at a higher rate than that of capital gains.

At the present time, if you charge less than 9 percent interest on your paper, the IRS will "impute" interest at a rate of 10 percent. In other words, the IRS will treat the transaction as if you were really receiving 10 percent interest. The following example demonstrates this catastrophe.

Assume that you agree to hold $50,000 in paper at 8 percent interest for twenty years. The monthly payments on that will be $418.23. The IRS will say this is really a 10 percent, $43,000 loan having approximately the same monthly payments. You will have to report over the life of the loan an additional $7,000 in interest ($50,000 - $43,000) that you had planned to either defer, exclude or report as nontaxable return of capital and/or favorably taxed capital gain.

Angry buyers and paper. One other thing about holding paper of any kind is that you had better tell your buyer anything that's wrong with your home, neighborhood, schools and so forth. Otherwise, you might find your buyer refusing to pay you because of your untruthfulness. This creates a Mexican standoff, in effect. The buyer owes you on the debt, but if you sue for it, you face a counter suit in fraud. I prefer the buyer's side in these cases.

As suggested earlier, it would be a very good idea for you to have a competent real estate lawyer at your side when you start talking about holding paper.

Recapping what has been said about holding paper is the following checklist.

Holding Paper Checklist

1. If the interest rate you will give is below market, raise your taking price and try to get a balloon payment, say three to five years out.
2. Do not obligate yourself to close until you are satisfied about your buyer's ability to pay you what is owed, when it's owed.
3. Secure your paper with a mortgage on your home or with other good collateral.
4. Require that the buyer provide hazard (disaster) insurance insuring you against fire or other hazards, credit

life insurance that will pay the loan off if the buyer (or the buyer's spouse) dies and mortgage insurance that will pay you off if the buyer defaults.

5. Include an alienation clause to restrict subsequent equity sales.
6. Include a stiff late payment penalty to encourage prompt payment.
7. Require that the buyer be personally liable, to discourage the buyer from walking off.
8. Get as large a down payment as possible for the same reason and to give you a cushion to fall back on.
9. Don't try to avoid an alienation clause in the senior mortgage.
10. Get the holder of any senior mortgage to agree to notify you in writing of your buyer defaulting and to allow you time to reinstate; or, alternatively, take back a wraparound so that you will know any senior mortgage is being paid.
11. Use a wraparound to increase your return.
12. Get your agent to agree to hold paper for part of the commission.
13. If you want to sell your paper, find out before you agree to anything with your buyer what you will be able to get for it, and how the lender wants the loan documents to be worded.
14. Don't get caught by the imputed interest rule.
15. Disclose to your buyer in writing anything about the home that you would want to know if you were buying it, or risk getting caught in a Mexican standoff.
16. Have the loan documents prepared before accepting the buyer's offer and attach them to the contract, initialed by you and the buyer.
17. Secure the services of a good residential real estate lawyer before doing anything.

13 *Contingency Offers*

A contingency offer is an escape hatch that allows the buyer to get out of the contract if some specified event does not occur. The most common contingency offers are those pertaining to the buyer selling a home, obtaining financing or inspecting the home. As stated earlier, an offer contingent on financing can be a sneaky way for a buyer to make an offer which is really contingent on selling a home.

Contingency offers are quite common, but they don't do much for you, especially in a buyer's market when homes aren't moving. In fact, they can really hurt you. Suppose, for example, you accept an offer contingent on the sale of the buyer's home. You have now tied up your property without knowing if you really have it sold.

Protective action. In view of the above, you should take protective action when presented with a contingency offer. Do not reduce your asking price or terms very much. Why should you? All you have been offered is a "maybe." Shorten the time for the buyer to do whatever it is the contingency calls for. Or, you could insist on the right to call off the deal if the contingency event hasn't occurred within a specified period of time. (This is what I renegotiated for The Elderly Couple.) I prefer the latter approach because it keeps the buyer on the hook until you decide to call off the deal.

Break clauses. Another way to improve a contingency offer is to put a break clause in your acceptance, which will give you the right to continue to show the home and get a better offer. Then, if you do get a better offer, your first buyer will either have to remove the contingency or agree to a cancellation of the contract. You can use a break clause any time the buyer makes a contingency offer. Break clauses are most often used, though, when a buyer makes an offer contingent on selling another home. The following is an example of this type of break clause:

> Seller may continue to show the home for sale. If Seller receives a more acceptable offer, then Seller may advise Buyer in writing of this fact. Buyer shall then have _____ hours to deliver to Seller in writing Buyer's agreement to remove the contingency about selling Buyer's home. If Buyer does not do this within the time allowed, Seller may void this contract by accepting the other offer and returning Buyer's earnest money.

Break clauses have their drawbacks, though. The main one is that other agents and buyers, who know there is a break clause contract, may not be very enthusiastic about seeing your home or making a serious offer, not knowing if you will be able to get out of the first contract. Also, you will probably find that the listing agent will not work as hard on selling your home after getting you a break clause contract. So your home is still taken off the market to some degree.

A way to minimize this problem is to instruct the listing agent not to tell anyone that a contract has been reached and not to report the contract to MLS. The agent may object to this. In fact, MLS rules in your area may require that the listing agent report the contract to MLS. Hold your ground. Point out to your agent that the contract is not firm and therefore does not really have to be reported. If this doesn't work, tell the agent you will not accept the offer if the agent will not agree to your request. Or, tell the agent you are going to cancel the listing after accepting the offer and then market the house yourself or through another firm. Be prepared to do this, too. If the listing agent believes you are serious, the thought of losing the commission or your home could create a remarkable attitude change.

If you are lucky enough to keep the contingency contract quiet, what do you do if you get another buyer's offer? That depends on whether or not the new offer suits you.

If you like the new offer (unlikely for an initial offer), stall accepting it until you know what the first buyer is going to do. Say you have to check with your wife, accountant, lawyer or whatever good excuse you can dream up. If the first buyer agrees to remove the contingency, tell the second buyer that you're sorry, but you have accepted another buyer's offer. If the first buyer declines to remove the contingency, accept the second buyer's offer and return the first buyer's earnest money.

In all probability, you will not like the second buyer's first offer and will want to make a counteroffer. Be careful here. While you don't want to tip your hand, you sure as heck don't want to sell the home twice and get sued by whichever buyer and agent lose out! There are two ways to approach the problem.

The first would be to reject the second buyer's offer but suggest *verbally* the price and terms you will accept. You cannot be bound by your verbal suggestion and, therefore, will not be in jeopardy of selling twice. The idea is to get the second buyer to make another, more acceptable *written* offer without the first contract being disclosed. This may look suspicious to the second buyer and queer the negotiations. However, the second buyer may make an offer you will accept. If that happens, proceed as outlined above.

The other way to approach this is to make a written counter-offer to the second buyer which is contingent on your being able to get out of the first contract. Now, the second buyer will know about the first contract. Will this cause the second buyer to get mad and withdraw from the negotiations? Perhaps. But the second buyer is now interested in your home. Whereas, if the second buyer or the co-op agent had known of the contingency contract, they may never have paid you a visit. If the second buyer sticks around and you reach an agreement (called a "back-up" contract), you proceed as outlined above.

Obviously, it will be easier on your nerves and less annoying to the new buyer for the break clause time to be relatively brief, twenty-four hours for example. If the first buyer lives out of town, twenty-four hours will still be reasonable, if you provide in the first contract that telegrams or cablegrams may serve as the required written notice from you and written response from the first buyer.

Liquidated damages. Another thing that you might ask for is a liquidated damages provision, stating you would get one-half of the earnest money (or some other sum) if the contingency event does not occur and the deal falls through. You will get raised eyebrows for suggesting this, but why should you take all the risks and the buyer none? A liquidated damages provision soothes the nerves.

* * * * *

The only time that accepting a contingency offer is completely safe is when you are a sell-first, buy-last person. Then you can afford to wait on the contingency to happen. If it doesn't, you haven't been hurt, because you can stay where you are.

14 *Earnest Money and Buyers with Cold Feet*

Earnest money (sometimes called the "binder" or "deposit") will probably be presented with the buyer's offer. This is a custom rather than a legal requirement showing the buyer's good faith. The earnest money is usually held by the listing broker or a neutral party. The amount of earnest money varies from place to place and deal to deal, and its purpose is to protect you if your buyer decides to break the contract. If that happens, you can keep the earnest money, but you may have other options.

Other legal remedies. Unless the contract states that the buyer's liability to you is limited to the earnest money or some other fixed amount, you can choose two other courses of action. The first is called "specific performance," which is a lawsuit where you ask the court to require the buyer to close. (This was what I threatened to do in the Nathans' case.) You may or may not succeed in getting such an order. If you don't, you will probably get an award for damages amounting to what the buyer's breaking the contract cost you. Alternatively, you can sell your home to someone else and sue the buyer for any loss you have incurred. Both approaches will require a lawyer's services.

Do *not* rely on the advice of your real estate agent, if your buyer breaks the contract. Instruct the listing and co-op agents not to have any further communication with the buyer. I have seen many cases, like the Nathans', where a buyer was, in fact, able to get out of a contract because of something the agent said, perhaps in an effort to stay on the buyer's good side and later close a sale with the buyer on someone else's home.

The more earnest money, the better. It probably would be best to get enough earnest money to protect you if the buyer breaks the contract. Then, you can afford to keep the earnest money and forget about the lawsuit. But keep in mind that the listing agreement your agent will ask you to sign or the form sales contract probably will have a provision saying that the agent and broker get part or all of the earnest money if a buyer breaks the contract. You should be able to negotiate this provision out of the listing agreement before giving the agent the listing or out of the sales contract before making a counter-offer. This early in the game, the agent and broker will be concentrating on getting a listing or selling your home and not on the remote possibility of a buyer backing out. Later, after it happens? Well, good luck!

Another thing about earnest money is that some buyers believe that a large amount of earnest money will cause you to lower your asking price. This is a consideration, if you are getting a no-nonsense, no-contingency offer. However, if you are getting a contingency offer without a liquidated damages provision, the amount of earnest money is irrelevant as long as the contingency is in place.

Who earns the interest? If there is a lot of earnest money involved, you may want it placed in an interest bearing account until the closing. The buyer will want the interest earned on the earnest money applied against, and you will want to add it onto, the purchase price. This is a negotiable point.

Deposit the check. One final thing about earnest money is that the buyer's check should be deposited as soon as the deal is made. I have known of many cases where the seller or agent "held" the buyer's earnest money check, then the buyer had a change-of-heart and stopped payment on it.

15 Little Things Can Hurt

Here are some little things which, like piranhas, have very big teeth.

Breach of contract expenses. In most states, you will not be entitled to recover your lawyer's fee or suit expenses if your buyer breaches the contract of sale, unless the sales contract provides that such costs shall be recoverable. This type of provision is a two-edged sword, meaning your buyer can use it to recover these costs from you, too, if you breach the agreement. An example of such a provision is:

> In the event of a breach of this agreement, the party not in breach shall be entitled to recover, in addition to any other damages, reasonable attorneys' fees and costs of litigation.

Although it is common to use such clauses in business agreements, I am not sure if it's a good idea to put something like this in a contract to sell a home. It looks so ominous. However, it might cause your buyer to think twice about suing you and losing. It has been my experience that 95 percent of the lawsuits concerning the sale of a home are initiated by the buyer. It has also been my experience that buyers win most of the suits.

Additional costs. There are additional costs that will have to be paid to get the deal closed, i.e., the loan fee and discount, lawyer's fee, survey, title insurance, etc.[1] Most of these can be paid by either the buyer or the seller, meaning they are negotiable. If the buyer is getting a new loan, the best way to handle closing costs is to add them onto the purchase price and then you agree to pay them, which enables the buyer to finance most of the costs and makes that amount available for the buyer's down payment.

Some costs you will have paid in advance and should either be refunded by your lender or reimbursed to you by the buyer at the closing. Examples of these costs are prepaid homeowner's and mortgage insurance premiums and, in some states, property taxes. If you have a mortgage on your home, then your lender probably has been requiring you to make advance payments into escrow (sometimes called the "impound") to make sure that there is enough money to pay your insurance premiums and property taxes when they next fall due. You will also be entitled to a refund or reimbursement for these escrowed costs at the closing.

Regardless of how closing costs, prepaid or escrowed items are to be handled, it is very important that you explain in the sales contract who is to pay what. Otherwise, you could end up taking a beating at the closing. With the movers on the way and your next home to close in an hour, you won't be in a very good position to argue.

Finally, if you have an FHA loan that will be paid off at the closing, send *written* notice of your intent to pay it off. The notice has to be *received* thirty days in advance, so give yourself time for slow mail or hand deliver it. This will save you thirty-days interest. You can save an additional thirty-days interest by closing and paying off the FHA loan before the

1. The Estimated Seller's Net form (Appendix D) contains the costs you are likely to encounter and shows how to compute them and your net.

first of the month. State in the sales contract a closing date which will allow time to mail or hand deliver the money to your lender before the first of the next month.

Delivery of possession. You will probably continue to live in your home until some time after closing. At least, I hope that you do. Any buyer that gets into your home before the closing will pick it apart and cause you a lot of problems. If you must let the buyer move in prior to closing, use a written "move-in" agreement prepared by a lawyer and require that the balance of the buyer's down payment be paid before occupancy.

The next consideration is timing your move out with your move into your next residence. Whether you will be leasing or buying, it may be difficult for you to precisely time the two events. I like the following contract wording for this problem:

> Seller will deliver possession on or before _____ or when Seller's next residence is ready for occupancy, whichever event last occurs.

Be prepared to show your buyer a copy of the contract or lease on your next residence, which will prove that you already have a place to go.

Another consideration is how much time you will need to move out after the closing. The longer you have been living in your home, the longer it will take you to get ready to move (remember The Elderly Couple's predicament). You shouldn't plan to move or do anything else permanent, like a large moving sale, before the closing. First, this puts you in a weak position with the buyer and opens the door for the buyer to try to take advantage of you. Second, if the buyer backs out at the last minute, you will have a real mess on your hands. And, if you go to the closing with the movers coming the next day, you will be in no position to be patient and wait out the buyer if a last minute problem develops.

In other words, leave yourself enough time to maneuver and state in the sales contract what your moving date will be. It would not be unreasonable for your buyer to require rent, if you are to stay longer than three or four days after the closing, and it will be worth your while to agree to this request.

Buyer protection provisions in the sales contract. Often, buyers put provisions in their offers which obligate you to them after the closing for problems that they do not discover until after moving in. Here is a simplified version of a clause I like to use for buyers:

> Seller promises Buyer that there is nothing seriously wrong with the home, or its systems and appliances, unless specifically stated in this contract.

You can see the danger to you of agreeing to such a provision, especially if you will be holding paper from the buyer. However, you are the one who has been living in the home and are in the best position to know what is wrong with it. So, this is not an unreasonable request on the buyer's part. You can limit such a provision by rewording it to say "to the best of Seller's knowledge there is nothing seriously wrong, given the age of the home and its systems," and by limiting the time that you are responsible for your promise. It will be much safer for you, though, to get the buyer to agree that the home is being sold "as is."

You will see other protective provisions, too, such as a right to inspect. These are also reasonable, but should be limited in time so as to not be open-ended. Something like this would suit you:

> The sale is contingent on a satisfactory inspection, the inspection to be deemed satisfactory unless Buyer notifies Seller otherwise in writing within ten days from the final signing of this contract.

This way, you aren't left dangling until the contract expiration date to find out that the inspection is or isn't satisfactory. At that point in time, a canny buyer may be able to get you to make substantial concessions to get the inspection contingency waived and the deal closed.

Another consideration is to use the buyer's protective provisions as negotiating chips. The more protection the buyer asks for, the less you reduce your price. Let the buyer know that you are selling this protection as part of the purchase price.

Good funds at closing. I have seen cases where the buyer wrote a personal check at the closing and stopped payment on it afterward. The way to avoid this is to require in the contract of sale that the buyer pay with "good funds," such as a cashier's or certified check. This also eliminates the closing agent requiring that no moneys be disbursed or documents recorded until the buyer's check has cleared the bank.

Removable property. Unless the contract of sale says otherwise, you can take any removable property with you when you move out. By removable property, I mean such things as the refrigerator, window air-conditioning units, area rugs, drapes and other such personal things, the removal of which do not damage or alter the real estate or home. You cannot remove things like the central vacuum system, built-in appliances, kitchen cabinets you had custom made and the dining room chandelier, unless the sales contract says that you can. Does this mean you automatically get your children's swing set or the dog pen in the back yard? I don't know. To be safe, state in the sales contract anything you plan to take with you that pertains to your home.

The Statute of Frauds. The "Statute of Frauds" is an ancient rule of law that says that agreements to sell or buy real estate must be in writing, else they are void. That's all there is to it. So, anything that you and the buyer have agreed to must be put in the contract of sale, which must be signed by all parties to be bound by it. Any changes made in the buyer's original offer must also be initialed by everyone. Then the final, signed and initialed agreement (or a copy of it) must be delivered to you and the buyer to seal the deal. It would be a good idea to have a lawyer review the final contract. It has been my experience that most agents are a poor choice to see that this is done properly.

Agreements with your real estate agent or the lender, on the other hand, do not have to be in writing, but they sure are hard to prove if they aren't. So put them in writing and deliver them, too.

Time is of the essence. These are magic words and are a trap for the unwary. They mean simply that the closing must occur on the date stated in the sales contract, failing which, the party not able to close is in breach of contract. Without these magic words in the contract of sale, the courts of most states have held that the closing only has to occur within a "reasonable" time after the stated closing date. This could be a week, a month or even later, depending on the facts and the disposition of the judge the day the case is heard. Of course, it might be months before the judge even hears the case at all.

I have often used this rule to stall closings for buyers who wanted a little more time to close. If you want to be assured of the right to close on the date agreed, write "time is of the essence" into your contract of sale. If you think *you* might need more time, then leave it out.

These magic words have also been held to apply to whether or not a loan must be promptly paid. If you are to hold paper and want the right to insist on prompt payment, write "time will be of the essence on the payments under the paper that Seller will hold" in your sales contract and tell your lawyer to put this wording into your paper.

* * * * *

Now you have made a deal and dodged most of the problems that can happen to a seller. Don't let down your guard, though, because it's not over yet.

16 *After Making the Deal*

After you have a signed contract, the burden shifts to the buyer to make arrangements to purchase your home. If you are working with an agent, the agent will assist the buyer with obtaining financing, hiring inspectors, obtaining insurance and so on. If you are not using an agent, then you will have to get involved in this, to make sure that the buyer keeps moving forward.

There will also be certain other things to do in order to get ready for the closing. They will be done by your agent; otherwise, you and the buyer will have to see to getting these things done. I am talking about such things as selecting a closing agent, ordering the title work, survey or fulfilling the requirements of a commercial lender.

If you are not using an agent, it would be a good idea to have a lawyer advising you what to do and making sure that it gets done right. You do not want to go to the closing with something left undone that will delay or kill the deal.

The inspection. After the deal is struck and the contract signed, the buyer and any commercial lender making the buyer a new loan will inspect the home. What do you do if, after the inspection is made, the buyer or lender asks you to make repairs?

Unless you have agreed to make repairs, you don't have to

do anything. But neither does the lender, and, if the buyer has an inspection contingency, neither does the buyer. So you have the makings for a beautiful Mexican standoff between you, the buyer and your agent(s). Forget the lender—he won't play this inning of the game.

There are several possible ways to resolve this: Wait and hope that the buyer is anxious and will absorb the costs (this will not work with a VA loan under which a buyer cannot pay repair costs); pay for the repairs yourself; ask your agent to pay for the repairs or work out a compromise as to who will bear what part of the costs. This is when the "secret" reimbursement for repairs agreement previously discussed will come in real handy—if you got it in writing.

I use this late-in-the game renegotiating technique for buyers quite often. You can guard against it by using a repair reimbursement agreement, being patient and waiting out the buyer and agent and by leaving yourself a little more room to negotiate when you make the initial deal.

Disaster insurance. What happens it, after signing the contract to sell your home, it burns down? You had better have it insured against hazards such as fire, storm and wind for what your buyer agreed to pay for it. Here's why.

Your sales contract probably will have a provision in it saying that you are required to insure your buyer's interest in the home until the closing. If you don't and the buyer cannot find another home like yours for the same price, then the buyer can sue you for damages. Most sellers carry homeowner's insurance, which contains hazard coverage. But often the coverage is for less than the sales price. If this is the situation in your case, the amount of coverage should be increased to an amount that will protect the buyer. This may be the sales price or even more, depending on the type of insurance you carry.

Suppose that the fire occurs after the closing but before you move out? The buyer now owns the home and will have insurance coverage on it. The buyer's coverage will not protect you, though, or your contents. So talk to your insurance agent before the closing about extending your contents and personal liability coverage until you have moved to your new home at which time your new homeowner's insurance will go into effect.

The closing. What you have read up to now will prepare you for why you bought this book—getting paid. If you are wondering why I am giving so little attention to the closing, it's because preparation is what really counts. The closing is just a routine event, if you have prepared properly. So, briefly, here's what you need to know about the closing.

Insist on seeing the closing documents a day or so before, so that you will have time to review them at your leisure. They will be unfamiliar to you, and the closing agent will move too fast for you to keep up if you haven't done your homework. If you have hired a lawyer, have him look over the closing documents, too. Do *not* go to the closing until you are satisfied that everything is in order. The closing is no place or time to be negotiating if you can avoid it.

The closing should now go smoothly. However, if an unexpected problem does come up, such as the buyer is short $500 but will have it for you next week, stop the closing until the matter is resolved to your satisfaction. If you have an agent, require that the agent's firm take a note from the buyer for the shortage and reduce the commission you owe by that amount. After all, the agent, not you, found the buyer, and the agent will not have earned the full commission until the buyer pays everything due you under the contract of sale. If you have allowed yourself some flexibility, you will be able to wait out the buyer and agent if such a last minute problem arises.

The closing agent will handle all of the paperwork, collection and paying of money. You should arrange with the buyer your moving date, delivery of the keys and transfer of utilities.

Once the closing is concluded, take the check that you will get from the closing agent to your bank and put the other documents in a nice, safe place, like a safety-deposit box. Then go home and start getting ready to move or look for another home, depending on whether you decided to buy first or last.

Conclusion

What I have written about selling a home leaves me with mixed feelings. Although I have given you many useful things, I wonder if I have made it even more difficult for my lambs, the buyers. I suppose, in a way, I have. But since most buyers are or will be sellers, in the long view I have also helped them.

I am thankful that I was fortunate to have the training and was in a position to expose the game and tell the people who have the most invested in it—buyers and sellers—how to play it. That was my goal.

Appendix A

STATE REAL ESTATE REGULATORY AGENCIES

ALABAMA
Real Estate Commission
State of Alabama
562 State Office Building
Montgomery, Alabama 36130
(205) 832-3266

ALASKA
Real Estate Commission of Alaska
Division of Occupational Licensing
Department of Commerce and Economic Development
Pouch D, Juneau, Alaska 99811
(907) 465-2500

ARIZONA
Arizona Department of Real Estate
1645 W. Jefferson Street
Phoenix, Arizona 85007
(602) 271-4345

ARKANSAS
Arkansas Real Estate Commission
101 Wallace Building
P.O. Box 3173
Little Rock, Arkansas 72203
(501) 371-1247

CALIFORNIA
Department of Real Estate
State of California
714 P Street
Sacramento, California 95814
(916) 445-8645

COLORADO
Colorado Real Estate Commission
110 State Services Building
1525 Sherman Street
Denver, Colorado 80203
(303) 892-2633

CONNECTICUT
Connecticut Real Estate Commission
90 Washington Street
Hartford, Connecticut 06115
(203) 566-5130

DELAWARE
Delaware Real Estate Commission
Division of Business and Occupational Regulations
Department of Administrative Services
State House Annex
Dover, Delaware 19901
(302) 678-4186

DISTRICT OF COLUMBIA
Real Estate Commission of the District of Columbia
Dept. of Economic Development
614 H Street, N.W.
Washington, D.C. 20001
(202) 629-4543

FLORIDA
Florida Real Estate Commission
400 West Robinson Avenue
Orlando, Florida 32801
(305) 423-6053

GEORGIA
Georgia Real Estate Commission
40 Pryor Street, S.W.
Atlanta, Georgia 30334
(404) 656-3916

HAWAII
Professional & Vocational
Licensing Division
Dept. of Regulatory Agencies
State of Hawaii
P.O. Box 3469
Honolulu, Hawaii 96801
(808) 548-7464

IDAHO
Idaho Real Estate Commission
633 North Fourth Street
State Capitol Building
Boise, Idaho 83720
(208) 384-3285

ILLINOIS
Dept. of Registration & Education
628 East Adams Street
Springfield, Illinois 62786
(217) 782-8024

INDIANA
Indiana Real Estate Commission
1022 State Office Building
100 North Senate Avenue
Indianapolis, Indiana 46204
(317) 633-5386

IOWA
Iowa Real Estate Commission
1223 East Court
Des Moines, Iowa 50319
(515) 281-3183

KANSAS
Kansas Real Estate Commission
Room 1212
535 Kansas Avenue
Topeka, Kansas 66603
(913) 296-3411

KENTUCKY
Kentucky Real Estate
Commission
100 E. Liberty Street, Suite 204
Louisville, Kentucky 40202
(502) 588-4462

LOUISIANA
Real Estate Commission
Dept. of Occupational Standards
P.O. Box 44517
Baton Rouge, Louisiana 70804
(504) 389-7755

MAINE
Maine Real Estate Commission
Dept. of Business Regulation
State Office Annex
Augusta, Maine 04333
(207) 289-3735

MARYLAND
Maryland Real Estate
Commission
Dept. of Licensing and
Regulation
1 South Calvert Street
Baltimore, Maryland 21202
(301) 383-2130

MASSACHUSETTS
Massachusetts Dept. of Civil Service and Registration
Board of Registration of Real Estate Brokers & Salesmen
Leverett Saltonstall Building
100 Cambridge Street
Boston, Massachusetts 02202
(617) 727-3055

MICHIGAN
Michigan Dept. of Licensing and Regulation, Real Estate Division
808 Southland
P.O. Box 30018
Lansing, Michigan 48909
(517) 373-0490

MINNESOTA
Commissioner of Securities
Department of Commerce
State of Minnesota
Metro Sq. Building, 5th Floor
St. Paul, Minnesota 55101
(612) 296-6319

MISSISSIPPI
Mississippi Real Estate Commission
Busby Building
754 North President
Jackson, Mississippi 39202
(601) 354-7093

MISSOURI
Missouri Real Estate Commission
3253 North 10 Mile Drive
P.O. Box 1339
Jefferson City, Missouri 65101
(314) 751-2334

MONTANA
Montana Real Estate Commission
La Londe Building
42½ North Main Street
Helena, Montana 59601
(406) 449-2961

NEBRASKA
Nebraska Real Estate Commission
2300 State Capitol Building
Lincoln, Nebraska 68509
(402) 471-2004

NEVADA
Administrator
Real Estate Division
Department of Commerce
Capitol Complex
201 South Fall Street, Room 129
Carson City, Nevada 89710
(702) 885-4280

NEW HAMPSHIRE
New Hampshire Real Estate Commission
3 Capitol Street
Concord, New Hampshire 03301
(603) 271-2701

NEW JERSEY
New Jersey Real Estate Commission
Department of Insurance
P.O. Box 1510
201 East State Street
Trenton, New Jersey 08625
(609) 292-7656

NEW MEXICO
New Mexico Real Estate
Commission
600 Second, N.W., Suite 608
Albuquerque, New Mexico 87102
(505) 842-3226

NEW YORK
Secretary of State
Department of State
Division of Licensing Services
162 Washington Avenue
Albany, New York 12231
(518) 474-2121

NORTH CAROLINA
North Carolina Real Estate
Licensing Board
115 Hillsborough Street
P.O. Box 266
Raleigh, North Carolina 27602
(919) 833-2771

NORTH DAKOTA
North Dakota Real Estate Comm.
410 East Thayer Avenue
P.O. Box 727
Bismarck, North Dakota 58505
(701) 224-2749

OHIO
Department of Commerce
Real Estate Commission
180 East Broad Street
Columbus, Ohio 43215
(616) 466-4100

OKLAHOMA
Oklahoma Real Estate
Commission
Suite 100
4040 North Lincoln Boulevard
Oklahoma City, Oklahoma 73105
(405) 521-3387

OREGON
Department of Commerce
Real Estate Division
158 12th Street, N.E.
Salem, Oregon 97310
(503) 378-4170

PENNSYLVANIA
Commissioner of Professional &
Occupational Affairs
State Real Estate Commission
Commonwealth of Pennsylvania
Box 2649
Harrisburg, Pennsylvania 17120
(717) 787-2100

RHODE ISLAND
Department of Business
Regulation
Real Estate Division
State of Rhode Island
100 North Main Island
Providence, Rhode Island 02903
(401) 277-2255

SOUTH CAROLINA
South Carolina Real Estate
Commission
2221 Devine Street, Suite 530
Columbia, South Carolina 29205
(803) 758-3981

SOUTH DAKOTA
South Dakota Real Estate Comm.
P.O. Box 638
Pierre, South Dakota 57501
(605) 224-3600

TENNESSEE
Tennessee Real Estate
Commission
556 Capitol Hill Building
Nashville, Tennessee 37219
(615) 741-2273

TEXAS
Texas Real Estate Commission
P.O. Box 12188
Capitol Station
Austin, Texas 78711
(512) 475-4250

UTAH
Real Estate Division
Department of Business
Regulation
State of Utah
330 East 4th South Street
Salt Lake City, Utah 84111
(801) 533-5661

VERMONT
Vermont Real Estate Commission
7 East State Street
Montpelier, Vermont 05602
(802) 828-3228

VIRGINIA
Dept. of Professional &
Occupational Regulation
Virginia Real Estate Commission
2 South 9th Street, 2nd Floor
P.O. Box 1-X
Richmond, Virginia 23202
(804) 786-2161

WASHINGTON
Business and Professions Admin.
Real Estate Division
P.O. Box 247
Olympia, Washington 98504
(206) 753-6681

WEST VIRGINIA
Real Estate Commission of West
Virginia
402 State Office Building No. 3
1800 East Washington Street
Charleston, West Virginia 25305
(304) 348-3555

WISCONSIN
Dept. of Regulation and
Licensing
Real Estate Examining Board
1400 East Washington Avenue
Madison, Wisconsin 53702
(608) 266-5450

WYOMING
Wyoming Real Estate
Commission
Supreme Court Building
Cheyenne, Wyoming 82002
(307) 777-7660

VIRGIN ISLANDS
Virgin Islands Real Estate
Commission
P.O. Box 925
Charlotte Amalie, St. Thomas
00801
(809) 774-2991

Appendix B

TYPICAL MULTIPLE LISTING SERVICE RULES AND REGULATIONS

LISTING PROCEDURES

Section 1 LISTING PROCEDURES: Listings of properties of the following types located within the territorial jurisdiction and marketing area of the Board of Realtors taken by Participants on an exclusive right to sell listing form shall be delivered to the Multiple Listing Service within 24 hours after necessary signatures of seller(s) have been obtained.

(a) Single-family homes for sale or exchange.
(b) Vacant lots and acreages for sale or exchange - optional.
(c) Investment or commercial properties - optional.

NOTE 1: Any participant may use an exclusive right to sell listing form for submission to the Multiple Listing Service. This means that a Multiple Listing Service should not require a Participant to submit the exclusive right to sell listings on a form other than the form the Participant individually chooses to utilize. However, the Multiple Listing Service, through its legal counsel:

1. May reserve the right to refuse to accept a listing form which fails to adequately protect the interest of the public and the Participants.

2. Assure that no listing form filed with the Multiple Listing Service establishes, directly or indirectly, any contractual relationship between the Multiple Listing Service and the client (buyer or seller).

The Multiple Listing Service, at its discretion, may accept in addition to exclusive right to sell listing contracts, other forms of agreement which make it possible for the listing broker to offer subagency to the other Participants of the Multiple Listing Service. The listing agreement must include the seller's authorization to submit the agreement to the Multiple Listing Service.

However, a "Property Data Form" shall be required as approved by the Multiple Listing Service.

NOTE 2: A Multiple Listing Service shall not regulate the type of listings its Members may take. This does not mean that a Multiple Listing Service must accept every type of listing. The Multiple Listing Service shall decline to accept open listings and net listings or even exclusive agency listings, subject to the provisions of the footnote related to Section 1.7, and it may limit its service to exclusive right to sell listings and even to listings of certain kinds of property. But if it chooses to limit the kind of listings it will accept, it shall leave its members free to accept such listings to be handled outside the Multiple Listing Service.

Section 1.1 LISTING SUBJECT TO RULES AND REGULATIONS OF THE SERVICE: Any listing taken on a contract to be filed with the Multiple Listing Service is subject to the Rules and Regulations of the Service upon signature of the seller(s).

Section 1.2 DETAIL ON LISTINGS FILED WITH THE SERVICE: A Listing Agreement or Property Data Form, when filed with the Multiple Listing Service by the listing broker, shall be complete in every detail which is ascertainable as specified on the Property Data Form.

Section 1.3 EXEMPTED LISTINGS: If the seller refuses to permit the listing to be disseminated by the Service, the Realtor may then take an exclusive right to sell ("office exclusive") and such listing shall be filed with the Service but not disseminated to the Participants. Filing of the listing should be accompanied by certification signed by the seller that he does not desire the listing to be disseminated by the Service.

Section 1.4 CHANGE OF STATUS OF LISTING: Any change in listed price or other change in the original listing agreement shall be made only when authorized in writing by the seller and shall be filed with the Service by the next weekly time and day for submission of data to the Service after the authorized change is received by the listing broker.

Section 1.5 WITHDRAWAL OF LISTING PRIOR TO EXPIRATION: Listings of property may be withdrawn from the Multiple Listing Service by the listing broker before the expiration date of the listing agreement provided notice is filed with the Service including a copy of the agreement between the seller and the listing broker which authorized the withdrawal.

Section 1.6 CONTINGENCIES APPLICABLE TO LISTINGS: Any contingency or conditions of any term in a listing shall be specified and noticed to the Participants.

Section 1.7 LISTING PRICE SPECIFIED: The full gross listing price should be stated in the contract. The Multiple Listing Service shall not accept net listing, open listings or exclusive agency listings.

NOTE: Acceptance of net listings and open listings would be inconsistent with the function of the MLS to facilitate the establishment of a subagency relationship between the listing and cooperating Participants since such listings do not by their nature authorize the listing broker to appoint subagents.

Section 1.8 LISTING MULTIPLE UNIT PROPERTIES: All properties which are to be sold or which may be sold separately must be indicated individually in the listing and on the Property Data Form. When part of a listed property has been sold, proper notification should be given to the Multiple Listing Service.

Section 1.9 NO CONTROL OF COMMISSION RATES OR FEES CHARGED BY PARTICIPANTS: The Multiple Listing Service shall not fix, control, recommend, suggest, or maintain commission rates or fees for services to be rendered by Participants. Further, the Multiple Listing Service shall not fix, control, recommend, suggest or maintain the division of commissions of fees between cooperating Participants or between Participants and nonparticipants.

Section 1.10 EXPIRATION, EXTENSION, AND RENEWAL OF LISTINGS: Any listing filed with the Multiple Listing Service automatically expires on the dates specified in the agreement unless renewed by the listing broker and notice of renewal or extension is filed with the Service prior to expiration.

Section 1.11 TERMINATION DATE ON LISTINGS: Listings filed with the Service shall bear a definite and final termination date as negotiated between the listing broker and seller.

Section 1.12 JURISDICTION: Only listings of the designated types of property located within the jurisdiction and market area of the Board of Realtors are required to be submitted to the Service. Listings of property located outside the Board's jurisdiction and market area may be accepted if submitted voluntarily by a Participant, but cannot be required by the Service.

Section 1.13 LISTINGS OF SUSPENDED PARTICIPANT: When a Participant of the Service is suspended from the MLS all listings currently filed with the MLS by the suspended Participant shall, at the Participant's option, be retained in the Service until sold, withdrawn, or expired.

Section 1.14 LISTINGS OF EXPELLED PARTICIPANT: When a Participant of the Service is expelled from the MLS, all listings currently filed with the MLS shall, at the Participant's option, be retained in the Service until sold, withdrawn or expired, and shall not be renewed or extended by MLS beyond the termination of the listing agreement in effect when the expulsion became effective.

SELLING PROCEDURE

Section 2 Negotiations with the seller for the showing and/or the purchase of listed property filed with MLS shall be conducted through the listing broker except when the listing broker gives the selling broker specific authority to negotiate directly.

Section 2.1 Listing broker must make arrangements to present offer as soon as possible, or give the selling broker a satisfactory reason for not doing so.

Section 2.2 Listing office shall submit to its principal all written offers received prior to the time an offer is accepted by the principal.

Section 2.3 Representative of selling broker shall have the right to be present when offer is presented only if permitted by the listing broker.

Section 2.4 Sales shall be reported immediately to the MLS office by the listing office, except if negotiations were carried on under Section 2 hereof, then the selling broker may report, sending a copy thereof to the listing broker within 24 hours after acceptance.

Section 2.5 Listing broker shall report to the MLS office within 24 hours that a contingency on file with the MLS office has been fulfilled or renewed, or the agreement cancelled.

Section 2.6 Advertising of any listing by a participant, other than the listing office is permissible only with the consent of the listing office.

Section 2.7 Listing office shall report immediately to the MLS office at the time any pending sale is cancelled, and listing shall be reinstated immediately.

REFUSAL TO SELL

Section 3 If the owner of any listed property filed with MLS refused to accept a written offer on the terms and conditions stated in the listing, information shall be transmitted to MLS regarding status of the listing and this information shall be transmitted to the participants.

PROHIBITIONS

Section 4 Any listing filed with MLS shall not be made available to any nonparticipant in MLS without the consent of the listing broker.

Section 4.1 "For Sale" signs of listing broker only may be placed on a property the listing of which is filed with MLS except with consent of listing broker.

Section 4.2 No "Sold" sign other than that of listing broker shall be placed on property, the listing of which is filed with MLS, except with the consent of the listing broker.

Section 4.3 No solicitation of any kind shall be made for listing a property in MLS by other than the listing broker until the listing has expired.

DIVISION OF COMMISSIONS

Section 5 The listing broker shall specify, on each listing submitted to the MLS, compensation being offered to other MLS Participants for their services as subagents which is applicable to such listing.

Section 5.1 If a participant acts as a principal in listing or buying property through the MLS, he shall make known his interest and shall be on the same basis as if he were acting as agent.

Section 6. SUBAGENT COMPENSATION SPECIFIED ON EACH LISTING: The listing broker shall specify, on each listing filed with the Multiple Listing Service, the compensation offered to other Multiple Listing Service participants for their services as subagents in the sale of such listing.

NOTE 1: In filing a property with the Multiple Listing Service of a Board of Realtors, the Participant of the Service is making a blanket unilateral offer of subagency to the other MLS Participants, and shall therefore specify on each listing filed with the Service, the compensation being offered by the listing broker to the other MLS Participants. Specifying the compensation on each listing is necessary because the cooperating broker (subagent) has the right to know what his compensation shall be prior to his endeavor to sell.*

This shall not preclude the listing broker from offering any MLS Participant compensation other than the compensation indicated on his listings as published by the MLS provided the listing broker informs the other broker in writing in advance and provided that the modification in the specified compensation is not the result of any agreement among all or any other Participants in the Service.

The Board Multiple Listing Service shall not disclose in any way the total commission negotiated between the seller and the listing broker.

*NOTE: The compensation specified on listings filed with the Multiple Listing Service may appear in one of various forms. The essential and appropriate requirement by a Board Multiple Listing Service is that the information to be published shall clearly inform the Participants as to the compensation they will receive as subagents in cooperative transactions unless advised otherwise by the listing broker in writing in advance. The compensation specified on listings published by the MLS may be shown in one of the following forms:

1. By showing a percentage of the gross selling price.
2. By showing a definite dollar amount.

NOTE 2: The listing broker may, from time to time, adjust the compensation being offered to other Multiple Listing Service Participants for their services as subagents with respect to any listing by advance published notice to the Service so that all Participants will be advised.

NOTE 3: The Multiple Listing Service should make no rule on the division of commissions between the Participants and nonparticipants. This should remain solely the responsibility of the listing broker.

Section 6.1 PARTICIPANT AS PRINCIPAL: If a Participant or any licensee affiliated with a Participant has any interest in property, the listing of which is to be disseminated through the Multiple Listing Service, that person shall disclose that interest when the listing is filed with the Multiple Listing Service and such information shall be disseminated to all Multiple Listing Service Participants.

SERVICE CHARGES

Section 7 SERVICE FEES AND CHARGES: The following service charges for operation of the Multiple Listing Service are in effect to defray the costs of the Service and are subject to change from time to time in the manner prescribed:

(a) Initial Participation Fee: An applicant for participation in the Service shall pay an application fee of $50.00 with such fee to accompany the application.

(b) Annual Participation Fee: The annual participation fee of each Participant shall be $50.00.

COMPLIANCE WITH RULES

Section 8 COMPLIANCE WITH RULES: The following action may be taken for noncompliance with the rules:

(a) For failure to pay any service charge or fee within one month of the date due, and provided that at least ten days notice has been given, the Service shall be suspended until service charges of fees are paid in full.

(b) For failure to comply with any other rule, the provisions of Sections 10 and 10.1 shall apply.

MEETINGS

Section 9 MEETINGS OF THE MLS COMMITTEE: The Multiple Listing Service Committee shall meet for the transaction of business at a time and place to be determined by the Committee or at the call of the Chairman.

Section 9.1 MEETINGS OF MLS PARTICIPANTS: The Committee may call meetings of the Participants in the Service to be known as meetings of the Multiple Listing Service.

Section 9.2 CONDUCT OF THE MEETINGS: The Chairman shall preside at all meetings or, in his absence, a temporary Chairman from the membership of the Committee shall be named by the Chairman, or upon his failure to do so, by the Committee.

ENFORCEMENT OF RULES OR DISPUTES

Section 10 CONSIDERATION OF ALLEGED VIOLATIONS: The Committee shall give consideration to all written complaints from Participants having to do with violations of the Rules and Regulations.

Section 10.1 VIOLATIONS OF RULES AND REGULATIONS: If the alleged offense is a violation of the Rules and Regulations of the Service, and does not involve a charge of alleged professional misconduct or request for arbitration, it may be considered and determined by the Multiple Listing Service Committee, and if a violation is determined, the Committee may direct the imposition of sanction, provided the recipient of such sanction may appeal it to the Professional Standards Committee of the Board for a hearing by the Professional Standards Committee in accordance with the Bylaws of the Board of Realtors.

Section 10.2 COMPLAINTS OF PROFESSIONAL MISCONDUCT: All other complaints of professional misconduct shall be referred by the Committee to the Secretary of the Board of Realtors for appropriate action in accordance with the professional standards procedures established in the Board's Bylaws.

PUBLICATION AND INFORMATION

Section 11 CONFIDENTIALITY OF MLS INFORMATION: Any publications provided by the Multiple Listing Service to the Participants shall be considered official publications of the Service. Such publications shall be considered confidential and exclusively for the use of real estate personnel affiliated with the Participants authorized and qualified to act as subagents of the listing broker in the sale of property filed with the Service. It shall be the duty and responsibility of Participants to disclose or to disseminate such publications only to sales personnel qualified to act as their subagents. Real estate personnel shall not let the MLS book out of their personal control.

Section 11.1 MLS NOT RESPONSIBLE FOR ACCURACY OF INFORMATION: The information published and disseminated by the Service is communicated verbatum, without change by the Service, as filed with the Service by the Participant. The Service does not verify such information provided and disclaims any responsibility for its accuracy. Each Participant agrees to hold the Service harmless against any liability arising from any inaccuracy or inadequacy of the information such Participant provides.

CHANGES IN RULES AND REGULATIONS

Section 12 CHANGES IN RULES AND REGULATIONS: Changes in Rules and Regulations of the Multiple Listing Service may be made by a majority vote of the Members of the Multiple Listing Service Committee, subject to approval by the Directors of the Board of Realtors.

Appendix C

CODE OF ETHICS OF THE NATIONAL ASSOCIATION OF REALTORS®

Revised and approved by the delegate body of the association at its 67th annual convention November 14, 1974

Preamble . . .

Under all is the land. Upon its wise utilization and widely allocated ownership depend the survival and growth of free institutions and of our civilization. The REALTOR® should recognize that the interests of the nation and its citizens require the highest and best use of the land and the widest distribution of land ownership. They require the creation of adequate housing, the building of functioning cities, the development of productive industries and farms, and the preservation of a healthful environment.

Such interests impose obligations beyond those of ordinary commerce. They impose grave social responsibility and a patriotic duty to which the REALTOR® should dedicate himself, and for which he should be diligent in preparing himself. The REALTOR®, therefore, is zealous to maintain and improve the standards of his calling and shares with his fellow REALTORS® a common responsibility for its integrity and honor. The term REALTOR® has come to connote competency, fairness, and high integrity resulting from adherence to a lofty ideal of moral conduct in business relations. No inducement of profit and no instruction from clients ever can justify departure from this ideal.

In the interpretation of this obligation, a REALTOR® can take no safer guide than that which has been handed down through the centuries, embodied in the Golden Rule, "Whatsoever ye would that men should do to you, do ye even so to them."

Accepting this standard as his own, every REALTOR® pledges himself to observe its spirit in all of his activities and to conduct his business in accordance with the tenets set forth below.

Article 1—The REALTOR® should keep himself informed on matters affecting real estate in his community, the state, and nation so that he may be able to contribute responsibly to public thinking on such matters.

Article 2—In justice to those who place their interests in his care, the REALTOR® should endeavor always to be informed regarding laws, proposed legislation, governmental regulations, public policies, and current market conditions in order to be in a position to advise his clients properly.

Article 3—It is the duty of the REALTOR® to protect the public against fraud, misrepresentation, and unethical practices in real estate transactions. He should endeavor to eliminate in his community any practices which could be damaging to the public or bring discredit to the real estate profession. The REALTOR® should assist the governmental agency charged with regulating the practices of brokers and salesmen in his state.

Article 4—The REALTOR® should seek no unfair advantage over other REALTORS® and should conduct his business so as to avoid controversies with other REALTORS®.

Article 5—In the best interests of society, of his associates, and his own business, the REALTOR® should willingly share with other REALTORS® the lessons of his experience and study for the benefit of the public, and should be loyal to the Board of REALTORS® of his community and active in its work.

Article 6—To prevent dissension and misunderstanding and to assure better service to the owner, the REALTOR® should urge the exclusive listing of property unless contrary to the best interest of the owner.

Article 7—In accepting employment as an agent, the REALTOR® pledges himself to protect and promote the interests of the client. This obligation of absolute fidelity to the client's interests is primary, but it does not relieve the REALTOR® of the obligation to treat fairly all parties to the transaction.

Article 8—The REALTOR® shall not accept compensation from more than one party, even if permitted by law, without the full knowledge of all parties to the transaction.

Article 9—The REALTOR® shall avoid exaggeration, misrepresentation, or concealment of pertinent facts. He has an affirmative obligation to discover adverse factors that a reasonably competent and diligent investigation would disclose.

Article 10—The REALTOR® shall not deny equal professional services to any person for reasons of race, creed, sex, or country of national origin.

The REALTOR® shall not be party to any plan or agreement to discriminate against a person or persons on the basis of race, creed, sex, or country of national origin.

Article 11—A REALTOR® is expected to provide a level of competent service in keeping with the standards of practice in those fields in which the REALTOR® customarily engages.

The REALTOR® shall not undertake to provide specialized professional services concerning a type of property or service that is outside his field of competence unless he engages the assistance of one who is competent on such types of property or service, or unless the facts are fully disclosed to the client. Any person engaged to provide such assistance shall be so identified to the client and his contribution to the assignment should be set forth.

The REALTOR® shall refer to the Standards of Practice of the National Association as to the degree of competence that a client has a right to expect the REALTOR® to possess, taking into consideration the complexity of the problem, the availability of expert assistance, and the opportunities for experience available to the REALTOR®.

Article 12—The REALTOR® shall not undertake to provide professional services concerning a property or its value where he has a present or contemplated interest unless such interest is specifically disclosed to all affected parties.

Article 13—The REALTOR® shall not acquire an interest in or buy for himself, any member of his immediate family, his firm or any member thereof, or any entity in which he has a substantial ownership interest, property listed with him, without making the true position known to the listing owner. In selling property owned by himself, or in which he has any interest, the REALTOR® shall reveal the facts of his ownership or interest to the purchaser.

Article 14—In the event of a controversy between REALTORS® associated with different firms, arising out of their relationship as REALTORS®, the REALTORS® shall submit the dispute to arbitration in accordance with the regulations of their board or boards rather than litigate the matter.

Article 15—If a REALTOR® is charged with unethical practice or is asked to present evidence in any disiplinary proceeding or investigation, he shall place all pertinent facts before the proper tribunal of the member board or affiliated institute, society, or council of which he is a member.

Article 16—When acting as agent, the REALTOR® shall not accept any commission, rebate, or profit on expenditures made for his principal-owner, without the principal's knowledge and consent.

Article 17—The REALTOR® shall not engage in activities that constitute the unauthorized practice of law and shall recommend that legal counsel be obtained when the interest of any party to the transaction requires it.

Article 18—The REALTOR® shall keep in a special account in an appropriate financial institution, separated from his own funds, monies coming into his possession in trust for other persons, such as escrows, trust funds, clients' monies, and other like items.

Article 19—The REALTOR® shall be careful at all times to present a true picture in his advertising and representations to the public. He shall neither advertise without disclosing his name nor permit any person associated with him to use individual names or telephone numbers, unless such person's connection with the REALTOR® is obvious in the advertisement.

Article 20—The REALTOR®, for the protection of all parties, shall see that financial obligations and commitments regarding real estate transactions are in writing, expressing the exact agreement of the parties. A copy of each agreement shall be furnished to each party upon his signing such agreement.

Article 21—The REALTOR® shall not engage in any practice or take any action inconsistent with the agency of another REALTOR®.

Article 22—In the sale of property which is exclusively listed with a REALTOR®, the REALTOR® shall utilize the services of other brokers upon mutually agreed upon terms when it is in the best interests of the client.

Negotiations concerning property which is listed exclusively shall be carried on with the listing broker, not with the owner, except with the consent of the listing broker.

Article 23—The REALTOR® shall not publicly disparage the business practice of a competitor nor volunteer an opinion of a competitor's transaction. If his opinion is sought and if the REALTOR® deems it appropriate to respond, such opinion shall be rendered with strict professional integrity and courtesy.

Article 24—The REALTOR® shall not directly or indirectly solicit the services or affiliation of an employee or independent contractor in the organization of another REALTOR® without prior notice to said REALTOR®.

Where the word REALTOR® is used in this Code and Preamble, it shall be deemed to include REALTOR-ASSOCIATE®. Pronouns shall be considered to include REALTORS® and REALTOR-ASSOCIATE®s of both genders.

The Code of Ethics was adopted in 1913. Amended at the Annual Convention in 1924, 1928, 1950, 1951, 1952, 1955, 1956, 1961, 1962, and 1974.

STANDARDS OF PRACTICE RELATING TO ARTICLES OF THE CODE OF ETHICS

(Adopted through November 17, 1981)

The Standards of Practice relating to the Code of Ethics are "interpretations" of various Articles of the Code of Ethics and are not a part of the Code itself. The proper relationship between the Standards of Practice and the Code of Ethics is set forth in the following advisory opinion by the Professional Standards Committee, which was approved by the Board of Directors of the National Association:

> In filing a charge of an alleged violation of the Code of Ethics by a REALTOR®, the charge shall read as an alleged violation of one or more Articles of the Code. A Standard of Practice may only be cited in support of the charge.

The Standards of Practice are supplementary to, and do not replace, the "numbered cases" found in *Interpretations of the Code of Ethics.* A Standard of Practice is a statement of general principle related to an Article of the Code of Ethics to guide REALTORS® and REALTOR-ASSOCIATE®s as to the professional conduct required in the specific situation described by the Standard of Practice, whereas each of the "numbered cases" in *Interpretations of the Code of Ethics* presents a set of particular facts alleging a violation of the Code of Ethics, and describes the conclusion determined on merit by the Professional Standards Committee as related to the particular facts of the case.

As additional Standards of Practice are adopted, Member Boards and Board Members will be advised of their adoption.

Standard of Practice 4-1—"The REALTOR® shall not misrepresent the availability of access to show or inspect a listed property."

Standard of Practice 7-1—"The REALTOR® shall receive and shall transmit all offers on a specified property to the owner for his decision, whether such offers are received from a prospective purchaser or another broker."

Standard of Practice 7-2—"The REALTOR®, acting as listing broker, shall submit all offers to the seller as quickly as possible."

Standard of Practice 7-3—"The REALTOR®, in attempting to secure a listing, shall not deliberately mislead the owner as to market value."

Standard of Practice 7-4—(Refer to Standard of Practice 22-1, which also relates to Article 7, Code of Ethics.)

Standard of Practice 7-5—(Refer to Standard of Practice 22-2, which also relates to Article 7, Code of Ethics.)

Standard of Practice 7-6—The REALTOR®, when acting as a principal in a real estate transaction, cannot avoid his responsibilities under the Code of Ethics.

Standard of Practice 9-1—"The REALTOR® shall not be a party to the naming of a false consideration in any document, unless it be the naming of an obviously nominal consideration."

Standard of Practice 9-2—"The REALTOR®, when asked by another REALTOR®, shall disclose the nature of his listing, i.e., an exclusive right to sell, an exclusive agency, open listing, or other form of contractual agreement between the REALTOR® and his client."

Standard of Practice 9-3—(Refer to Standard of Practice 7-3, which also relates to Article 9, Code of Ethics.)

Standard of Practice 9-4—"The REALTOR® shall not offer a service described as 'free of charge' when the rendering of a service is contingent on the obtaining of a benefit such as a listing or commission."

Standard of Practice 9-5—"The REALTOR® shall, with respect to the subagency of another REALTOR®, timely communicate any change of compensation for subagency services to the other REALTOR® prior to the time such REALTOR® produces a prospective buyer who has signed an offer to purchase the property for which the subagency has been offered through MLS or otherwise by the listing agency."

Standard of Practice 9-6—REALTORS® shall disclose their REALTOR® status when seeking information from another REALTOR® concerning real property for which the other REALTOR® is an agent or subagent.

Standard of Practice 11-1—"Whenever a REALTOR® submits an oral or written opinion of the value of real property for a fee, his opinion shall be supported by a memorandum in his file or an appraisal report, either of which shall include as a minimum the following:

1. Limiting conditions
2. Any existing or contemplated interest
3. Defined value
4. Date applicable
5. The estate appraised
6. A description of the property
7. The basis of the reasoning including applicable market data and/or capitalization computation

"This report or memorandum shall be available to the Professional Standards Committee for a period of at least two years (beginning subsequent to final determination of the court if the appraisal is involved in litigation) to ensure compliance with Article 11 of the Code of Ethics of the NATIONAL ASSOCIATION OF REALTORS®."

Standard of Practice 11-2—"The REALTOR® shall not undertake to make an appraisal when his employment or fee is contingent upon the amount of appraisal."

Standard of Practice 11-3—"REALTORS® engaged in real estate securities and syndications transactions are engaged in an activity subject to regulations beyond those governing real estate transactions generally, and therefore have the affirmative obligation to be informed of applicable federal and state laws, and rules and regulations regarding these types of transactions."

Standard of Practice 12-1—(Refer to Standard of Practice 9-4, which also relates to Article 12, Code of Ethics.)

Standard of Practice 15-1—"The REALTOR® shall not be subject to disciplinary proceedings in more than one Board of REALTORS® with respect to alleged violations of the Code of Ethics relating to the same transaction."

Standard of Practice 16-1—"The REALTOR® shall not recommend or suggest to a principal or a customer the use of services of another organization or business entity in which he has a direct interest without disclosing such interest at the time of the recommendation or suggestion."

Standard of Practice 19-1—"The REALTOR® shall not submit or advertise property without authority, and in any offering, the price quoted shall not be other than that agreed upon with the owners."

Standard of Practice 19-2—(Refer to Standard of Practice 9-4, which also relates to Article 19, Code of Ethics.)

Standard of Practice 21-1—"Signs giving notice of property for sale, rent, lease, or exchange shall not be placed on property without the consent of the owner."

Standard of Practice 21-2—"The REALTOR® obtaining information from a listing broker about a specific property shall not convey this information to, nor invite the cooperation of a third party broker without the consent of the listing broker."

Standard of Practice 21-3—"The REALTOR® shall not solicit a listing which is currently listed exclusively with another broker unless the listing broker, when asked by the REALTOR®, refuses to disclose the nature and current status of such listing; i.e., an exclusive right to sell, an exclusive agency, open listing, or other form of contractual agreement between the REALTOR® and his client."

Standard of Practice 21-4—"The REALTOR® shall not use information obtained by him from the listing broker, through offers to cooperate received through Multiple Listing Services or other sources authorized by the listing broker, for the purpose of creating a referral prospect to a third broker, or for creating a buyer prospect unless such use is authorized by the listing broker."

Standard of Practice 21-5—"The fact that a property has been listed exclusively with a REALTOR® shall not preclude or inhibit any other REALTOR® from soliciting such listing after its expiration."

Standard of Practice 21-6—"The fact that a property owner has retained a REALTOR® as his exclusive agent in respect of one or more past transactions creates no interest or agency which precludes or inhibits other REALTORS® from seeking such owner's future business."

Standard of Practice 21-7—"The REALTOR® shall be free to solicit a listing in respect to any property which is 'open listed' at any time."

Standard of Practice 21-8—"Unless otherwise precluded by law, the REALTOR® may discuss with an owner of a property which is exclusively listed with another REALTOR® the terms upon which he would accept a future listing upon the expiration of the present listing provided the owner initiates the discussion and provided the REALTOR® has not directly or indirectly solicited such discussion."

Standard of Practice 21-9—"In cooperative transactions a REALTOR® shall compensate the cooperating REALTOR® (principal broker) and shall not compensate nor offer to compensate, directly or indirectly, any of the sales licensees employed by or affiliated with another REALTOR® without the prior express knowledge and consent of the cooperating broker."

Standard of Practice 22-1—"It is the obligation of the selling broker as subagent of the listing broker to disclose immediately all pertinent facts to the listing broker prior to as well as after the contract is executed."

Standard of Practice 22-2—"The REALTOR®, when submitting offers to the seller, shall present each in an objective and unbiased manner."

Standard of Practice 24-1—"The purpose of Article 24 is to discourage salespersons from breaching their agreements with the REALTORS® by whom they are employed or with whom they are affiliated. Its further purpose is to prevent REALTORS® from inducing salespersons to breach such agreements.

"Article 24 must not be construed as precluding a REALTOR® from making an offer of employment or affiliation to the salesperson of another REALTOR® at any time or on any terms he deems appropriate. Any use of Article 24 to limit the opportunities for employment or affiliation available to salespersons is improper and a violation of Article 24.

"Article 24 is infringed only in the case where a REALTOR® solicits the services of a specific employee or independent contractor salesperson or another REALTOR® who is under a written agreement. A general announcement by a REALTOR® that he is interested in expanding his staff and invites qualified persons to call or write him is not a solicitation violative of Article 24. Nor would a REALTOR® be required by Article 24 to notify the REALTOR® with whom salespersons responding to such general announcement are associated."

Appendix D

ESTIMATED SELLER'S NET

Assumed selling price		$ ________
Plus amount in escrow (impound)		________
Total purchase price		________
Less expenses		________
Survey	________	
Title insurance/lawyer's opinion	________	
Closing agent's fee	________	
Commission	________	
Prepayment penalty	________	
Loan fee	________	
Discount	________	
Assumption fee	________	
Termite/pest inspection/guarantee	________	
Recording fees	________	
Appraisal/inspection	________	
Credit report	________	
Lender required repairs	________	

Total expenses	________	
Prorations		
Property taxes	________	
Interest	________	
Insurance	________	
Association dues	________	
Garbage/sewer fee	________	
Utilities	________	
Other	________	
Total expenses		________
Net before mortgages		________
Less		
First mortgage balance	________	
Second mortgage balance	________	
Total mortgages		________
Approximate net to seller		________

Appendix E

SAMPLE GRIEVANCE COMPLAINT

TO: REAL ESTATE COMMISSION (OR BOARD OF REALTORS®)

OF ______________________

COMPLAINT

IN THE MATTER OF

______________________ ______________________

Complainant Address

AGAINST

______________________ ______________________

Name of Agent/Broker Address of Agent/Broker

Complainant alleges the following facts against the above named agent/broker and states that, to the best of Complainant's knowledge, said allegations are true.

The said agent/broker did the following acts on or about the ________ day of ______________, 19________:

Complainant believes that said alleged acts violated the real estate licensing laws of this state (or the Code of Ethics and Standards of Practice of the Board of Realtors®).

Therefore, Complainant asks that an appropriate investigation be conducted as to the allegations made above.

____

Complainant

STATE OF ______________________

COUNTY OF ____________________

Personally appeared before the undersigned authority the complainant named in the foregoing complaint, who on oath says that the facts stated above are true to the best of the complainant's knowledge.

____

Complainant

Sworn to and subscribed before me this the ________ day of ____________, 19________.

____

Notary Public

Index

Agent. *See* Real estate agent
Alienation clause
  defined, 25
  Fannie Mae, 25
  FHA, 25
  holding paper and, 30
  how to handle, 26
  Paragraph, 17, 25
  penalties, 26
  VA, 25
  wraparound mortgage and, 82
Appraisal
  buyer's offer, 76
  by agent, 56
  by owner, 57
  by purchasing company, 46
  by residential appraiser, 53, 56
  drawbacks, 56
Asking price, 55
Attorney. *See* Lawyer

Breach of contract expenses, 97
Break clause
  contingency clause, 90
  defined, 44, 90
  drawbacks, 90
Broker
  as advisor, 38
  commissions, 15, 66
  defined, 15
  listing agreement with, 64
Buy-downs, 53
Buyer
  disclosures to, 11, 12
  financing, 27
  games, 12
  holding paper from, 27, 79
  negotiations, 74
  personal check, 101
  protection plans, 52
  protective provisions in buyer's offer, 100
  researching, 74
  wariness, 11
Buyer's market
  contingency offer in, 89
  defined, 47
  high interest rates in, 47
  holding paper, 79
Buyer-paid agent
  commission, 68
  explained, 68
  hourly rate, 69
  referral service, 71

Closing
  agent, 35
  costs, 98, 134

documents, 107
funds, 101
stalling at, 102
Closing agent
allegiance, 35
defined, 35
lawyers as, 35
responsibilities of, 35
Closing costs
defined, 31
example of, 32
financing the, 32
in general, 98
payment of, 98
points, 31
Seller's Net form, 134
tax deductible, 31
Code of Ethics, 125
Commercial lenders, 31
Commission
attempts to avoid, 64
broker/agent split, 15
broker's approval, 66
buyer-paid agent, 68
For Sale By Owner homes, 59
negotiating, 65
net listing, 64
Contingency offer
buyer's market, 89
counteroffers to, 91
dealing with, 89
defined, 89
liquidated damages provision, 92
Contingency clause, 90
Contract negotiations
counteroffers, 75
face-to-face, 75
offers, 69, 73
patience, 76
researching the buyer, 74
written requirements, 69, 102
Co-oping the commission
defined, 18
double agent, 18
FTC, 18
protection against, 21
Counteroffer
asking price, 75
defined, 75
holding paper, 75
taking price, 75
to contingency offer, 91
Credit life insurance, 30

Deed of trust. *See* Mortgage
Disclaimer, author's, x
Disclosure requirements, 11
Discount broker, 65
Double agent
Board of Realtors®, 19
co-oping, 18
defined, 17
fiduciary duty, 17
NAR, 19
penalties for breach of, 20

Earnest money
amount of, 94
defined, 93
interest on, 94
Estimated Seller's Net form, 134

Factor table, 29
Federal Housing Administration (FHA) loans
alienation clauses, 25
prepayment penalties, 23, 98
repairs, 33
to pay off, 98

Federal National Mortgage
Association (Fannie Mae), 25
Federal/state taxes, 45
Federal Trade Commission (FTC)
co-oping, 37
study, 18
Fiduciary duty
breach of, 20
buyer information, 74
defined, 16
double agent, 17
listing agent, 16, 67
For Sale By Owner homes
buyer reaction, 60
commission, 59
multiple listing service for, 60
reasons against, 59
using a lawyer, 60

Grievance complaint form, 137
Guaranteed purchase plan, 46

Holding paper
agents, 66
alienation clause, 30
balloon arrangement, 28, 80
buyer's market, 79
checklist, 86
counteroffers, 75
defined, 27
protective steps, 80
real estate agents, 29
retaining title, 82
sellers, 29
seller's market, 79
selling paper, 84
wraparound mortgage, 81
Home loans, 23
House condition, 51
House defects
agents and, 12
disclosure to buyer of, 11
sellers and, 11

Inspection
buyer's, 105
repairs, 105
sales tool, 52
Interest
effect on price, 58, 83
imputed interest rule, 85
in buyer's market, 47
mortgage prepayment, 24
on earnest money, 94
Insurance
credit life, 30
disaster, 30, 106
mortgage, 30

Job-related moves, 45

Lawyer
as advisor, 38
as closing agent, 35
breach of contract expenses, 97
fees, 39
For Sale By Owner homes, 60
holding paper, 31, 87
locating, 39
Paragraph 17 mortgages, 26
specific performance, 93
Liquidated damages provision, 92
Listing agreement, 64

Mortgage
assumable, 52
insurance, 30
payoff, 53

prepayment penalties, 23
second, 28
senior, 30
wraparound, 81
Multiple Listing Service (MLS)
defined, 16
For Sale By Owner homes, 60
rules and regulations, 117

National Association of Realtors®
(NAR)
Code of Ethics, 17, 125
double agents, 19
members, 16
Realtors®, 15

Paragraph 17 mortgage
alienation clauses, 25
defined, 25
Fannie Mae, 25
Points
defined, 31
example of, 32
tax deductible, 31
VA loans, 32
Prepayment penalties
FHA, 23
interest, 24
mortgage payoff, 53
VA, 23
waived, 24
Price
affected by, 58
appraisals, 56
asking, 56
bargaining, 55
counteroffers, 75
determining value, 55
taking, 55
Principal, 85
Property taxes, 98

Real estate agent
as advisor, 38
broken contracts, 94
buying and selling, 67
co-oping, 18
disclosure of defects, 12
fiduciary duty, 16
full-time, 63
house defects, 12
licensing, 15
Realtor®, 15
selecting one, 63
seller's responsibility for, 20
steering, 64
with large firm, 64
Realtor®, 15
Regulatory agencies, 111

Seller financing. *See* Holding paper
Seller's market
defined, 47
holding paper in, 79
offers in, 76
Specific performance, 93
State real estate regulatory
agencies, 111
Statute of Frauds, 102
Survey, 51

Taking price, 55
Tax deduction, 44
Tax on sale, 45
Time of essence, 102
Title, 51
Trust deed. *See* Mortgage

Veterans Administration (VA) loans
alienation clauses, 25
discount points, 32
house repairs, 33
prepayment penalties, 23

Wraparound mortgage
alienation clause, 82
balloon payment, 82
extra return on, 88
holding paper, 81